Paulo Coelho

Like the Flowing River

Thoughts and Reflections

Translated from the Portuguese by
Margaret Jull Costa

HARPER

HARPER

HarperCollins*Publishers*
77–85 Fulham Palace Road,
Hammersmith, London W6 8JB

HarperCollins' website address is:
www.harpercollins.co.uk
Paulo Coelho's website address is:
www.paulocoelho.com

First published in English by HarperCollins*Publishers* 2006

13 5 7 9 10 8 6 4 2

A catalogue record of this book
is available from the British Library

ISBN-13 978-0-00-723579-7
ISBN-10 0-00-723579-8

Printed and bound in Great Britain by
Clays Ltd, St Ives plc

Mixed Sources
Product group from well-managed
forests and other controlled sources
www.fsc.org   Cert no. SW-COC-1806
© 1996 Forest Stewardship Council
FSC

Be like the flowing river,
Silent in the night.
Be not afraid of the dark.
If there are stars in the sky, reflect them back.
If there are clouds in the sky,
Remember, clouds, like the river, are water,
So, gladly reflect them too,
In your own tranquil depths.

Manuel Bandeira

Contents

Preface

When I was fifteen, I said to my mother: 'I've discovered my vocation. I want to be a writer.'

'My dear,' she replied sadly, 'your father is an engineer. He's a logical, reasonable man with a very clear vision of the world. Do you actually know what it means to be a writer?'

'Being someone who writes books.'

'Your Uncle Haroldo, who is a doctor, also writes books, and has even published some. If you study engineering, you can always write in your spare time.'

'No, Mama. I want to be a writer, not an engineer who writes books.'

'But have you ever met a writer? Have you ever seen a writer?'

'Never. Only in photographs.'

'So how can you possibly want to be a writer if you don't really know what it means?'

In order to answer my mother's question, I decided to do some research. This is what I learned about what being a writer meant in the early 1960s:

(a) A writer always wears glasses and never combs his hair. Half the time he feels angry about everything and the other half depressed. He spends most of his life in bars, arguing with other dishevelled, bespectacled writers. He says very 'deep' things. He always has amazing ideas for the plot of his next novel, and hates the one he has just published.

(b) A writer has a duty and an obligation never to be understood by his own generation; convinced, as he is, that he has been born into an age of mediocrity, he believes that being understood would mean losing his chance of ever being considered a genius. A writer revises and rewrites each sentence many times. The vocabulary of the average man is made up of 3,000 words; a real writer never uses any of these, because there are another 189,000 in the dictionary, and he is not the average man.

(c) Only other writers can understand what a writer is trying to say. Even so, he secretly hates all other writers, because they are always jockeying for the same vacancies left by the history of literature over the centuries. And so the writer and his peers compete for the prize of 'most complicated book': the one who wins will be the one who has succeeded in being the most difficult to read.

(d) A writer understands about things with alarming names, like semiotics, epistemology, neoconcretism. When he wants to shock someone, he says things like: 'Einstein is a fool', or 'Tolstoy was the clown of the bourgeoisie'. Everyone is scandalized, but they nevertheless go and tell other people that the theory of relativity is bunk, and that Tolstoy was a defender of the Russian aristocracy.

(e) When trying to seduce a woman, a writer says: 'I'm a writer', and scribbles a poem on a napkin. It always works.

(f) Given his vast culture, a writer can always get work as a literary critic. In that role, he can show his generosity by writing about his friends' books. Half of any such reviews are made up of quotations from foreign authors and the other half of analyses of sentences, always using expressions such as 'the epistemological cut', or 'an integrated bi-dimensional vision of life'. Anyone reading the review will say: 'What a cultivated person', but he won't buy the book because he'll be afraid he might not know how to continue reading when the epistemological cut appears.

(g) When invited to say what he is reading at the moment, a writer always mentions a book no one has ever heard of.

(h) There is only one book that arouses the unanimous admiration of the writer and his peers: *Ulysses* by James Joyce. No writer will ever speak ill of this book, but when someone asks him what it's about, he can't quite explain, making one doubt that he has actually read it.

Armed with all this information, I went back to my mother and explained exactly what a writer was. She was somewhat surprised.

'It would be easier to be an engineer,' she said. 'Besides, you don't wear glasses.'

However, I did already have the untidy hair, a packet of Gauloises in my pocket, the script of a play under my arm (*The Limits of Resistance*, which, to my delight, a critic described as 'the maddest thing I've ever seen on stage'); I was also studying Hegel and was determined, somehow or other, to read *Ulysses*. Then a rock singer turned up and asked me to write words for his songs, and I withdrew from the search for immortality and set myself once more on the same path as ordinary people.

This path took me to many places and caused me to change countries more often than I changed shoes, as Bertolt Brecht used to say. The pages that follow contain accounts of some of my own experiences, stories other people have told me, and thoughts I've had while travelling down particular stretches of the river of my life.

These stories and articles have all been published in various newspapers around the world and have been collected together at the request of my readers.

Like the Flowing River

A Day at the Mill

At the moment, my life is a symphony composed of three distinct movements: 'a lot of people', 'a few people', and 'almost no one'. Each of them lasts about four months of the year; and although there is often a little of each during one particular month, they never get confused.

'A lot of people' is when I'm in touch with the public, with publishers and journalists. 'A few people' happens when I go back to Brazil, meet up with old friends, stroll along Copacabana beach, go to the occasional social event, but mostly stay at home.

What I want to do today, though, is to talk a little about the 'almost no one' movement. Right now, night has fallen on the two hundred inhabitants of this Pyrenean village, whose name I prefer to keep secret and where, a short while ago, I bought a converted mill. I wake every morning at cock-crow, have breakfast, and go out for a walk amongst the cows and the sheep and the fields of maize and hay. I look at the mountains and – unlike during the 'a lot of people' movement – I never think about who I am. I have no questions and no answers; I live entirely in the present moment, knowing that the year has four seasons (yes, I know this may seem obvious, but we do sometimes forget), and I transform myself just as the countryside does around me.

At the moment, I'm not much interested in what's going on in Iraq or in Afghanistan: like anyone else living in the country, the most important news is the weather forecast. Everyone who lives in the small village knows whether it's going to rain, whether it will be cold or very windy, since this directly affects their lives, their plans, their harvests. I see a farmer working in his field. We wish each other 'Good morning', discuss the likely weather, and then go on with what we were doing – he with his ploughing, me with my long walk.

I come back, look in the letter-box, and there's the local newspaper: a dance in the neighbouring village; a lecture in a bar in Tarbes – the nearest big city with its forty thousand inhabitants; last night, the fire brigade was called out because a litter bin was set on fire. The subject agitating the region at the moment is a group thought to be responsible for cutting down a line of plane trees along a country road because they blame the trees for the death of a motorcyclist. This news takes up a whole page, and there are several days' worth of articles about the 'secret cell' that wants to avenge the boy's death by destroying the trees.

I lie down by the stream that runs past the mill. I look up at the cloudless sky in this terrifying summer, during which the heatwave has killed five thousand in France alone. I get up and go and practise kyudo, a form of meditation through archery, and this takes up another hour of my day. It's lunchtime now; I have a light meal and then, in one of the other rooms in the old building, I suddenly notice a strange object, with a screen and a keyboard, connected – marvel of marvels

– by a high-speed line, also known as a DSL. I know that the moment I press a button on that machine, the world will come to meet me.

I resist as long as I can, but the moment arrives, my finger presses the on-switch, and here I am again connected with the world: Brazilian newspapers, books, interviews to be given, news about Iraq, about Afghanistan, requests, a note that my plane ticket will arrive tomorrow, decisions to be postponed, decisions to be taken.

I work for several hours, because that is my choice, because that is my personal legend, because a warrior of light knows that he has duties and responsibilities. But during the 'almost no one' movement, everything on the computer screen seems very far away, just as this mill seems like a dream when I'm caught up in the other movements – 'a lot of people' and 'a few people'.

The sun is setting. I switch the computer off again, and the world goes back to being the countryside, the smell of grass, the lowing of cattle, the voice of the shepherd bringing his sheep back to the pen beside the mill.

I ask myself how I can exist in two such different worlds in one day. I have no answer, but I know that it gives me a great deal of pleasure, and that I am happy while I write these lines.

Prepared for Battle, But With a Few Doubts

I'm wearing a strange green outfit, full of zips, and made from a very tough fabric. I have gloves on, too, in order to avoid cuts and scratches. I'm carrying a kind of spear, almost as tall as I am. The metal end has three prongs on one side, and a sharp point on the other.

And before me lies the object of my attack: the garden.

With the spear in my hand, I start to remove the weeds growing amongst the grass. I do this for quite a while, knowing that each plant I dig up will die within two days.

Suddenly, I ask myself: am I doing the right thing?

What we call a 'weed' is, in fact, an attempt at survival by a particular species that took Nature millions of years to create and develop. The flower was fertilized at the expense of innumerable insects; it was transformed into seed; the wind scattered it over the fields round about; and so – because it was not planted in just one place, but in many – its chances of surviving until next spring are that much greater. If it was concentrated in just one place, it would be vulnerable to being eaten, to flood, fire and drought.

But all that effort to survive is brought up short by the point of a spear, which mercilessly plucks the plant from the soil.

Why am I doing this?

Someone created this garden. I don't know who, because when I bought the house, the garden was already here, in harmony with the surrounding mountains and trees. But its creator must have thought long and hard about what he or she was doing, must have carefully planted and planned (for example, there is an avenue of trees that conceals the hut where we keep the firewood) and tended it through countless winters and springs. When I moved into the old mill – where I spend a few months of each year – the lawn was immaculate. Now it is up to me to continue that work, although the philosophical question remains: should I respect the work of the creator, of the gardener, or should I accept the survival instinct with which nature endowed this plant, which I now call a 'weed'?

I continue digging up unwanted plants and placing them on a pile that will soon be burned. Perhaps I am giving too much thought to things that have less to do with thought and more to do with action. But, then, every gesture made by a human being is sacred and full of consequences, and that makes me think even more about what I am doing.

On the one hand, these plants have the right to broadcast themselves everywhere. On the other hand, if I don't destroy them now, they will end up choking the grass. In the New Testament, Jesus talks about separating the wheat from the tares.

But – with or without the support of the Bible – I am faced by a concrete problem always faced by humanity: how far should we interfere with nature? Is such interference always negative, or can it occasionally be positive?

I set aside my weapon – also known as a weeder. Each blow means the end of a life, the death of a flower that would have bloomed in the spring – such is the arrogance of the human being constantly trying to shape the landscape around him. I need to give the matter more thought, because I am, at this moment, wielding the power of life and death. The grass seems to be saying: 'If you don't protect me, that weed will destroy me.' The weed also speaks to me: 'I travelled so far to reach your garden. Why do you want to kill me?'

In the end, the Hindu text, the *Bhagavad-Gita* comes to my aid. I remember the answer that Krishna gives to the warrior Arjuna, when the latter loses heart before a decisive battle, throws down his arms, and says that it is not right to take part in a battle that will culminate in the death of his brother. Krishna says, more or less: 'Do you really think you can kill anyone? Your hand is My hand, and it was already written that everything you are doing would be done. No one kills and no one dies.'

Encouraged by this recollection, I pick up my spear again, attack the weeds I did not invite to grow in my garden, and am left with this morning's one lesson: when something undesirable grows in my soul, I ask God to give me the same courage mercilessly to pluck it out.

The Way of the Bow

The importance of repetition

An action is a thought made manifest.

The slightest gesture betrays us, so we must polish everything, think about details, learn the technique in such a way that it becomes intuitive. Intuition has nothing to do with routine, but with a state of mind that is beyond technique.

So, after much practising, we no longer think about the necessary movements: they become part of our own existence. But for this to happen, you must practise and repeat.

And if that isn't enough, you must repeat and practise.

Look at a skilled farrier working steel. To the untrained eye, he is merely repeating the same hammer blows; but anyone who follows the way of the bow, knows that each time the farrier lifts the hammer and brings it down, the intensity of the blow is different. The hand repeats the same gesture, but as it approaches the metal, it understands that it must touch it with more or less force.

Look at a windmill. To someone who glances at its sails only once, they seem to be moving at the same speed, repeating the same movement; but those familiar with windmills know that they are controlled by the wind and change direction as necessary.

The hand of the farrier was trained by repeating the gesture of hammering thousands of times. The sails of the windmill can move fast when the wind blows hard, and thus ensure that its gears run smoothly.

The archer allows many arrows to go far beyond the target, because he knows that he will only learn the importance of bow, posture, string and target, by repeating his gestures thousands of time, and by not being afraid to make mistakes.

And then comes the moment when he no longer has to think about what he is doing. From then on, the archer becomes his bow, his arrow and his target.

How to observe the flight of the arrow

The arrow is the projection of an intention into space.

Once the arrow has been shot, there is nothing more the archer can do, except follow its path to the target. From that moment on, the tension required to shoot the arrow has no further reason to exist. Therefore, the archer keeps his eyes fixed on the flight of the arrow, but his heart rests, and he smiles.

If he has practised enough, if he has managed to develop his instinct, if he has maintained elegance and concentration throughout the whole process of shooting the arrow, he will, at that moment, feel the presence of the universe, and will see that his action was just and deserved.

Technique allows the hands to be ready, the breathing to be precise, and the eyes to be trained on the target. Instinct allows the moment of release to be perfect.

Anyone passing nearby, and seeing the archer with his arms open, his eyes following the arrow, will think that nothing is happening. But his allies know that the mind of the person who made the shot has changed dimensions: it is now in touch with the whole universe. The mind continues to work, learning all the positive things about that shot, correcting possible errors, accepting its good qualities, and waiting to see how the target reacts when it is hit.

When the archer draws the bow-string, he can see the whole world in his bow. When he follows the flight of the arrow, that world grows closer to him, caresses him and gives him a perfect sense of duty fulfilled.

A warrior of light, once he has done his duty and transformed his intention into gesture, need fear nothing else: he has done what he should have done. He did not allow himself to be paralysed by fear. Even if the arrow failed to hit the target, he will have another opportunity, because he did not give in to cowardice.

The Story of the Pencil

A boy was watching his grandmother write a letter. At one point, he asked:

'Are you writing a story about what we've done? Is it a story about me?'

His grandmother stopped writing her letter and said to her grandson:

'I *am* writing about you, actually, but more important than the words is the pencil I'm using. I hope you will be like this pencil when you grow up.'

Intrigued, the boy looked at the pencil. It didn't seem very special.

'But it's just like any other pencil I've ever seen!'

'That depends on how you look at things. It has five qualities which, if you manage to hang on to them, will make you a person who is always at peace with the world.

'First quality: you are capable of great things, but you must never forget that there is a hand guiding your steps. We call that hand God, and He always guides us according to His will.

'Second quality: now and then, I have to stop writing and use a sharpener. That makes the pencil suffer a little, but afterwards, he's much sharper. So you, too, must learn to bear certain pains and sorrows, because they will make you a better person.

'Third quality: the pencil always allows us to use an eraser to rub out any mistakes. This means that correcting something we did is not necessarily a bad thing; it helps to keep us on the road to justice.

'Fourth quality: what really matters in a pencil is not its wooden exterior, but the graphite inside. So always pay attention to what is happening inside you.

'Finally, the pencil's fifth quality: it always leaves a mark. In just the same way, you should know that everything you do in life will leave a mark, so try to be conscious of that in your every action.'

How to Climb Mountains

Choose the mountain you want to climb

Don't be influenced by what other people say: 'that one's prettier' or 'that one looks easier'. You are going to put a lot of energy and enthusiasm into achieving your objective, and you are the only person responsible for your choice, so be quite sure about what you are doing.

Find out how to reach the mountain

Often you can see the mountain in the distance – beautiful, interesting, full of challenges. However, when you try to reach it, what happens? It's surrounded by roads; forests lie between you and your objective; and what seems clear on the map is far more complicated in reality. So you must try all the paths and tracks until, one day, you find yourself before the peak you intend to climb.

Learn from someone who has been there before

However unique you may think you are, there is always someone who has had the same dream before, and who will have left signs behind that will make the climb less arduous: the best place to attach a rope, trodden paths, branches broken off to make it easier to pass. It is your climb and it is your responsibility too, but never forget that other people's experiences are always helpful.

Dangers, seen from close to, are controllable

When you start to climb the mountain of your dreams, pay attention to what is around you. There are, of course, precipices. There are almost imperceptible cracks. There are stones polished so smooth by rain and wind that they have become as slippery as ice. But if you know where you are putting your foot, you will see any traps and be able to avoid them.

The landscape changes, so make the most of it

You must, naturally, always keep in mind your objective – reaching the top. However, as you climb, the view changes, and there is nothing wrong with stopping now and then to enjoy the vista. With each metre you climb, you can see a little further, so take time to discover things you have never noticed before.

Respect your body

You will only manage to climb a mountain if you give your body the care it deserves. You have all the time that life gives you, so do not demand too much from your body. If you walk too quickly, you will grow tired and give up halfway. If you walk too slowly, night might fall and you will get lost. Enjoy the landscape, drink the cool spring water, and eat the fruit that Nature so generously offers you, but keep walking.

Respect your soul

Don't keep repeating, 'I'm going to do it.' Your soul knows this already. What it needs to do is to use this long walk in order to grow, to reach out as far as the horizon, to touch the sky. Obsession will not help you in the search for your goal, and will end up spoiling the pleasure of the climb. On the other hand, don't keep repeating 'It's harder than I thought,' because that will sap your inner strength.

Be prepared to go the extra mile

The distance to the top of the mountain is always greater than you think. There is bound to come a moment when what seemed close is still very far away. But since you are prepared to go still further, this should not be a problem.

Be joyful when you reach the top

Cry, clap your hands, shout out loud that you made it; let the wind (because it is always windy up there) purify your mind, cool your hot, weary feet, open your eyes, blow the dust out of your heart. What was once only a dream, a distant vision, is now part of your life. You made it, and that is good.

Make a promise

Now that you have discovered a strength you did not even know you had, tell yourself that you will use it for the rest of your days; promise yourself, too, to discover another mountain and set off on a new adventure.

Tell your story

Yes, tell your story. Be an example to others. Tell everyone that it's possible, and then others will find the courage to climb their own mountains.

The Importance of a Degree

My old mill, in a small village in France, has a line of trees that separates it from the farm next door. The other day, my neighbour came to see me. He must be about seventy years old. I've sometimes seen him and his wife working in the fields, and thought that it was high time they stopped.

My neighbour is a very pleasant man, but he says that the leaves from my trees are falling on his roof and that I should cut the trees down.

I'm really shocked. How can a person who has spent his entire life in contact with Nature want me to destroy something that has taken so long to grow, simply because, in ten years' time, it might cause problems with his roof?

I invite him in for a coffee. I say that I'll take full responsibility, and that if, one day, those leaves (which will, anyway, be swept away by the wind and by the summer) do cause any damage, I'll pay for him to have a new roof. My neighbour says that that doesn't interest him; he wants me to cut down those trees. I get slightly angry and say that I would rather buy his farm from him.

'My land isn't for sale,' he says.

'But with that money you could buy a lovely house in town and live out the rest of your days there with your wife, without having to put up with harsh winters and failed harvests.'

'My farm is not for sale. I was born here and grew up here, and I'm too old to move.'

He suggests that we get an expert from town to come and assess the situation and make a decision – that way, neither of us need get angry with the other. We are, after all, neighbours.

When he leaves, my first reaction is to label him as insensitive and lacking in respect for Mother Earth. Then I feel intrigued: why would he not agree to sell his land? And before the day is over, I realize that it is because his life has only one story, and my neighbour does not want to change that story. Going to live in the town would mean plunging into an unknown world with different values, and maybe he thinks he's too old to learn.

Is this something peculiar to my neighbour? No. I think it happens to everyone. Sometimes, we are so attached to our way of life that we turn down a wonderful opportunity simply because we don't know what to do with it. In his case, his farm and his village are the only places he knows, and there is no point in taking any risks. In the case of people who live in the town, they all believe that they must have a university degree, get married, have children, make sure that their children get a degree too, and so on and so on. No one asks themselves: 'Could I do something different?'

I remember that my barber worked day and night so that his daughter could finish her sociology degree. She finally graduated and, after knocking on many doors, found work as a secretary at a cement works. Yet my barber still used to say very proudly: 'My daughter's got a degree.'

Most of my friends, and most of my friends' children, also have degrees. That doesn't mean that they've managed to find the kind of work they wanted. Not at all. They went to university because someone, at a time when universities were important, said that, in order to rise in the world, you had to have a degree. And thus the world was deprived of some excellent gardeners, bakers, antique dealers, sculptors, and writers. Perhaps this is the moment to review the situation. Doctors, engineers, scientists, and lawyers need to go to university, but does everyone? I'll let these lines by Robert Frost provide the answer:

> *Two roads diverged in a wood, and I –*
> *I took the one less traveled by,*
> *And that has made all the difference.*

Just to conclude the story about my neighbour. The expert came and, to my surprise, showed us a French law which states that any tree has to be at least three metres from another property. Mine are only two metres away, and so I will have to cut them down.

In a Bar in Tokyo

The Japanese journalist asks the usual question: 'Who are your favourite writers?'

And I give my usual answer: 'Jorge Amado, Jorge Luis Borges, William Blake and Henry Miller.'

The interpreter looks at me in amazement:

'Henry Miller?'

Then she realizes that it is not her role to ask questions, and she carries on interpreting. At the end of the interview, I ask her why she was so surprised by my response. Was it perhaps because Henry Miller is not considered to be 'politically correct'? He was someone who opened up a vast world for me, and his books have an energy and a vitality rarely found in contemporary literature.

'No, I'm not criticizing Henry Miller. I'm a fan of his too,' she said. 'Did you know that he was married to a Japanese woman?'

Of course I knew. I'm not ashamed to be enough of a fan to want to find out everything about a writer and his life. I went to a book fair once just to meet Jorge Amado; I travelled forty-eight hours in a bus to meet Borges (and it was my fault that I didn't, because when I saw him, I froze and couldn't say a word); I rang the bell of John Lennon's apartment in New York (the doorman asked me to leave a letter explaining the reason for my visit and said that John Lennon would phone me, but he never did); I had plans to go to Big Sur to see Henry Miller, but he died before I had saved enough money for the trip.

'The Japanese woman is called Hoki,' I said proudly. 'I also know that there is a museum of his watercolours in Tokyo.'

'Would you like to meet her tonight?'

What a question! Of course I would like to meet someone who once lived with one of my idols. I imagine she must receive visitors and requests for interviews from all over the world; after all, she lived with Miller for nearly ten years. Surely she won't want to waste her time on a mere fan? But if the translator says it's possible, I had better take her word for it – the Japanese always keep their word.

I spend the rest of the day anxiously waiting. We get into a taxi, and everything starts to seem very strange. We stop in a street where the sun probably never shines, because a railway viaduct passes right over it. The translator points to a second-rate bar on the second floor of a crumbling building.

We go up some stairs, enter a deserted bar, and there is Hoki Miller.

To conceal my surprise, I exaggerate my enthusiasm for her ex-husband. She takes me to a room in the back, where she has created a little museum – a few photos, two or three signed watercolours, a book with a dedication written in it, and nothing more. She tells me that she met him when she was studying for an MA in Los Angeles and that, in order to make ends meet, she used to play piano in a restaurant and sing French songs (in

Japanese). Miller had supper there once and loved the songs (he had spent much of his life in Paris); they went out a few times, and he asked her to marry him.

I see that there is a piano in the bar – as if she were returning to the past, to the day when they first met. She tells me some wonderful stories about their life together, about the problems that arose from the difference in their ages (Miller was over fifty, and Hoki not yet twenty), about the time they spent together. She explains that the heirs from his other marriages inherited everything, including the rights to the books, but that this didn't matter because the experience of being with him outweighed any monetary compensation.

I ask her to play the same song that first caught Miller's attention all those years ago. She does this with tears in her eyes, and sings 'Autumn Leaves' ('Feuilles mortes').

The translator and I are moved too. The bar, the piano, the voice of that Japanese woman echoing through the empty room, not caring about the success of the other ex-wives, or the rivers of money that must flow from Miller's books, or the international fame she could be enjoying now.

'There was no point in squabbling over the inheritance: love was enough,' she said at last, sensing what we were feeling. Yes, in the light of that complete absence of bitterness or rancour, I think love really was enough.

The Importance of Looking

At first, Theo Wierema was merely a very persistent individual. For five years, he kept sending letters to my office in Barcelona, inviting me to give a talk in The Hague, in Holland.

For five years, my office replied that my diary was full. My diary was not, in fact, always full, but a writer is not necessarily someone who speaks well in public. Besides, everything I need to say is in the books and articles I write, which is why I always try to avoid giving lectures.

Theo found out that I was going to record a programme for a Dutch television channel. When I went downstairs to start filming, he was waiting for me in the hotel lobby. He introduced himself and asked if he could go with me, saying: 'I'm not one of those people who simply won't take "No" for an answer; I think I may just be going the wrong way about achieving my goal.'

We must struggle for our dreams, but we must also know that, when certain paths prove impossible, it would be best to save our energies in order to travel other roads. I could have simply said 'No' (I have said and heard this word many times), but I decided to adopt a more diplomatic approach: I would impose conditions that would be impossible for him to meet.

I said that I would give the lecture for free, but the entrance fee must not exceed two euros, and the hall must contain no more than two hundred people.

Theo agreed.

'You're going to spend more than you're going to earn,' I warned him. 'By my calculation, the cost of the air ticket and hotel alone will cost three times what you will earn if you manage to fill the hall. Then there's the advertising and the hire of the hall ...'

Theo interrupted me, saying that none of this mattered. He was doing this because of what he could see happening in his work.

'I organize events like this because I need to keep believing that human beings are still in search of a better world. I need to contribute to making this possible.'

What was his work?

'I sell churches.'

And, to my amazement, he went on: 'I'm employed by the Vatican to select buyers, because there are more churches than there are church-goers in Holland. And since we've had some terrible experiences in the past, with sacred places being turned into nightclubs, condominiums, boutiques, and even sex-shops, the system of selling churches has changed. The project has to be approved by the community, and the buyer has to say what he or she is going to do with the building. We normally only accept proposals that include a cultural centre, a charitable institution, or a museum. And what has this to do with the lecture, and with the other events I'm trying to organize? People don't really meet together any more, and if they don't meet, they won't grow.'

Looking at me hard, he concluded: 'Meetings. That was the mistake I made with you. Instead of just sending e-mails, I should have shown you that I'm made of flesh and blood. Once, when I failed to get a reply from a particular politician, I went and knocked on his door, and he said to me: "If you want something, you need to look the other person in the eye." Ever since then, that's what I've done, and I've had nothing but good results. You can have at your disposal all the means of communication in the world, but nothing, absolutely nothing, can replace looking someone in the eye.'

Needless to say, I accepted his proposal.

P.S. When I went to The Hague to give the lecture, and knowing that my wife, who is an artist, has always wanted to set up a cultural centre, I asked to see some of the churches that were for sale. I asked the price of one which used to hold 500 parishioners every Sunday, and it cost one euro (ONE euro!), but the maintenance costs can reach prohibitive levels.

Genghis Khan and His Falcon

On a recent visit to Kazakhstan, in Central Asia, I had the chance to accompany some hunters who still use the falcon as a weapon. I don't want to get into a discussion here about the word 'hunt', except to say that, in this case, Nature was simply following its course.

I had no interpreter with me, but what could have been a problem turned out to be a blessing. Unable to talk to them, I paid more attention to what they were doing. Our small party stopped, and the man with the falcon on his arm remained a little way apart from us and removed the small silver hood from the bird's head. I don't know why he decided to stop just there, and I had no way of asking.

The bird took off, circled a few times, and then dived straight down towards the ravine and stayed there. When we got close, we found a vixen caught in the bird's talons. That scene was repeated once more during the morning.

Back at the village, I met the people who were waiting for me and asked them how they managed to train the falcon to do everything I had seen it do, even to sit meekly on its owner's arm (and on mine too; they put some leather armbands on me and I could see the bird's sharp talons close up).

It was a pointless question. No one had an explanation. They said that the art is passed from generation to generation – father trains son, and so on. But what will remain engraved for ever in my mind are the snowy mountains in the background, the silhouetted figures of horse and horseman, the falcon leaving the horseman's arm, and that deadly dive.

What also remains is a story that one of those people told me while we were having lunch.

One morning, the Mongol warrior, Genghis Khan, and his court went out hunting. His companions carried bows and arrows, but Genghis Khan carried on his arm his favourite falcon, which was better and surer than any arrow, because it could fly up into the skies and see everything that a human being could not.

However, despite the group's enthusiastic efforts, they found nothing. Disappointed, Genghis Khan returned to the encampment and in order not to take out his frustration on his companions, he left the rest of the party and rode on alone. They had stayed in the forest for longer than expected, and Khan was desperately tired and thirsty. In the summer heat, all the streams had dried up, and he could find nothing to drink. Then, to his amazement, he saw a thread of water flowing from a rock just in front of him.

He removed the falcon from his arm, and took out the silver cup which he always carried with him. It was very slow to fill and, just as he was about to raise it to his lips, the falcon flew up, plucked the cup from his hands, and dashed it to the ground.

Genghis Khan was furious, but then the falcon was his favourite, and perhaps it, too, was thirsty. He picked up the cup, cleaned off the dirt, and filled it again. When the cup was only half-empty this time, the falcon again attacked it, spilling the water.

Genghis Khan adored this bird, but he knew that he could not, under any circumstances, allow such disrespect; someone might be watching this scene from afar and, later on, would tell his warriors that the great conqueror was incapable of taming a mere bird.

This time, he drew his sword, picked up the cup and refilled it, keeping one eye on the stream and the other on the falcon. As soon as he had enough water in the cup and was ready to drink, the falcon again took flight and flew towards him. Khan, with one thrust, pierced the bird's breast.

The thread of water, however, had dried up; but Khan, determined now to find something to drink, climbed the rock in search of the spring. To his surprise, there really was a pool of water and, in the middle of it, dead, lay one of the most poisonous snakes in the region. If he had drunk the water, he, too, would have died.

Khan returned to camp with the dead falcon in his arms. He ordered a gold figurine of the bird to be made and on one of the wings, he had engraved:

Even when a friend does something you do not
like, he continues to be your friend.

And on the other wing, he had these words engraved:

Any action committed in anger is an action
doomed to failure.

Looking at Other People's Gardens

'You can give a fool a thousand intellects, but the only one he will want is yours,' says an Arabic proverb. When we start planting the garden of our life, we glance to one side and notice our neighbour is there, spying. He himself is incapable of growing anything, but he likes to give advice on when to sow actions, when to fertilize thoughts, and when to water achievements.

If we listen to what this neighbour is saying, we will end up working for him, and the garden of our life will be our neighbour's idea. We will end up forgetting about the earth we cultivated with so much sweat and fertilized with so many blessings. We will forget that each centimetre of earth has its mysteries that only the patient hand of the gardener can decipher. We will no longer pay attention to the sun, the rain, and the seasons; we will concentrate instead only on that head peering at us over the hedge.

The fool who loves giving advice on our garden never tends his own plants at all.

Pandora's Box

During the course of one morning, I receive three signs coming from different continents. An e-mail from the journalist, Lauro Jardim, asking me to confirm certain facts in a note about me, and mentioning the situation in Rocinha, Rio de Janeiro. A phone call from my wife, who has just landed in France. She had taken a couple who are friends of ours to Brazil to show them the country, and the couple had both ended up feeling both frightened and disappointed. Then the journalist who has come to interview me for a Russian television station asks me if it's true that in Brazil over half a million people were murdered between 1980 and 2000.

Of course it's not true, I say.

But then he shows me the statistics from 'a Brazilian institute' (the Brazilian Institute of Geography and Statistics as it turns out).

I fall silent. The violence in my country has crossed oceans and mountains and reached this place in Central Asia. What can I say?

Saying isn't enough, because words that are not transformed into actions 'breed pestilence', as William Blake said. I have tried to do my bit. I set up my institute, along with two heroic people, Isabella and Yolanda Maltarolli, where we try to give education, affection and love to 360 children from the Pavão-

Pavãozinho *favela* or shanty town. I know that, at this moment, thousands of Brazilians are doing much more: working away silently, without official help, without private support, merely in order not to be over-whelmed by that worst of all enemies – despair.

I used to think that if everyone played their part, then things would change; but tonight, while I look out at the icy mountains on the frontier with China, I have my doubts. Perhaps, even with everyone doing their bit, the saying I learned as a child is still true: 'You can-not argue with force.'

I look again at the mountains lit by the moon. Is it really true that against force there is no argument? Like all Brazilians, I tried and fought and struggled to believe that the situation in my country would, one day, get better; but with each year that passes, things only seem to grow more complicated, regardless of who the president is, which political party is in power, what their economic plans are, or, indeed, regardless of the absence of all these things.

I've witnessed violence in the four corners of the world. I remember once, in Lebanon, immediately after the devastating war there, I was walking amongst the ruins of Beirut with a friend, Söula Saad. She told me that her city had now been destroyed seven times. I asked, jokingly, why they didn't give up rebuilding it and move somewhere else. 'Because it's our city,' she replied. 'Because the person who does not honour the earth in which his ancestors are buried will be cursed for all eternity.'

The person who dishonours his country, dishonours himself. In one of the classic Greek creation myths,

Zeus, furious because Prometheus had stolen fire and thus given independence to mortal men, sends Pandora off to marry Prometheus' brother, Ephemetheus. Pandora takes with her a box which she has been forbidden to open. However, just as with Eve in Christian mythology, her curiosity gets the better of her. She lifts the lid to see what is inside and, at that moment, all the evils of the world fly out and scatter about the earth. Only one thing remains inside: hope.

So, despite the fact that everything contradicts this, despite my sadness and my feelings of impotence, despite being almost convinced at this moment that nothing will ever get better, I cannot lose the one thing that keeps me alive: hope – that word treated with such irony by pseudo-intellectuals, who consider it a synonym of 'deceit'. That word, so manipulated by governments, who make promises they know they will not keep, and thus inflict even more wounds on people's hearts. That word that so often rises with us in the morning, gets sorely wounded as the day progresses, dies at nightfall, and is reborn with the new day.

Yes, there is a saying that states that 'You cannot argue with force'; but there is another saying: 'Where there's life, there's hope.' And I hang on to that saying as I look across at the snowy mountains on the Chinese border.

How One Thing Can Contain Everything

A meeting in the house of a São Paulo-born painter based in New York. We are talking about angels, and about alchemy. At one point, I try to explain to the other guests the alchemical idea that each of us contains the whole universe and that we are, therefore, responsible for its well-being. I struggle to find the right words, but cannot come up with a good image that will explain my point of view.

The painter, who has been listening in silence, asks everyone to look out of the window of his studio.

'What can you see?' he asks.

'A street in Greenwich Village,' someone replies.

The painter sticks a piece of paper over the window so that the street can no longer be seen; then, with a penknife, he cuts a small square in the paper.

'And if someone were to look through there, what would he see?'

'The same street,' comes the reply.

The painter cuts several squares in the paper.

'Just as each of these holes contains within it the whole view of the same street, so each of us contains in our soul the same universe,' he says.

And all of us applaud the lovely image he has found.

The Music Coming From the Chapel

On the day of my birthday, the universe gave me a present which I would like to share with my readers.

In the middle of a forest near the small town of Azereix, in south-west France, there is a tree-covered hill. With the temperature nudging 40°C, in a summer when nearly five thousand people have died in hospital because of the heat, we look at the fields of maize almost ruined by the drought, and we don't much feel like walking. Nevertheless, I say to my wife:

'Once, after I dropped you off at the airport, I decided to explore this forest. I found a really pretty walk. Would you like me to show you?'

Christina sees something white in the middle of the trees and asks what it is.

'It's a hermitage,' I say, and tell her that the path passes right by it, but that on the one occasion I was there, the hermitage was closed. Accustomed as we are to the mountains and the fields, we know that God is everywhere and that there is no need for us to go into a man-made building in order to find him. Often, during our long walks, we pray in silence, listening to the voice of nature, and understanding that the invisible world always manifests itself in the visible world. After a half-hour climb, the hermitage appears before us in the middle of the wood, and the usual questions arise. Who built it? Why? To which saint is it dedicated?

And as we approach, we hear music and singing, a single voice that seems to fill the air about us with joy. 'The other time I was here, there weren't any loud-speakers,' I think, finding it strange that someone should be playing music to attract visitors on such a little-used track.

But this time, the door of the hermitage is open. We go in, and it is like entering a different world: the chapel lit by the morning light; an image of the Immaculate Conception on the altar; three rows of pews; and, in one corner, in a kind of ecstasy, a young woman of about twenty, playing her guitar and singing, with her eyes fixed on the image before her.

I light three candles, as I usually do when I enter a church for the first time (one for me, one for my friends and readers, and one for my work). I look back. The young woman has noticed our presence, but she simply smiles and continues playing.

A sense of paradise seems to descend from the heavens. As if she understood what was going on in my heart, the young woman combines music with silence, now and again pausing to say a prayer.

And I am aware that I am experiencing an unforgettable moment in my life, the kind of awareness we often only have once the magic moment has passed. I am entirely in the moment, with no past, no future, merely experiencing the morning, the music, the sweetness, the unexpected prayer. I enter a state of worship and ecstasy, and gratitude for being alive. After many tears, and what seems to me an eternity, the young woman stops playing. My wife and I get up and thank her. I say that I would like to send her a present for having filled my soul with peace that morning. She says that she goes there every morning and that this is her way of praying. I insist that I would like to give her a present. She hesitates, but finally gives me the address of a convent.

The following day, I send her one of my books and, shortly afterwards, receive a reply, in which she says that she left the hermitage that day with her soul flooded with joy, because the couple who came in had shared her worship and shared, too, in the miracle of life.

In the simplicity of that small chapel, in the young woman's voice, in the morning light that filled everything, I understood once again that the greatness of God always reveals itself in the simple things.

The Devil's Pool

I'm looking at a lovely natural pool near the village of Babinda in Australia. A young Aborigine comes over to me.

'Be careful you don't slip,' he says.

The small pool is surrounded by rocks, apparently quite safe to walk on.

'This place is called the Devil's Pool,' the boy goes on. 'Many years ago, Oolona, a beautiful Aborigine girl who was married to a warrior from Babinda, fell in love with another man. They fled into these mountains, but the husband found them. The lover escaped, but Oolona was murdered here in these waters. Ever since then, Oolona thinks that every man who comes near is her lost love, and she kills him with her watery embrace.'

Later on, I ask the owner of the small hotel about the Devil's Pool.

'It might just be superstition,' he says, 'but the fact is that eleven tourists have died there in the last ten years, and they were all men.'

The Dead Man Wore Pyjamas

I read in an on-line newspaper on the internet that, on 10 June 2004, in Tokyo, a man was found dead in his pyjamas.

So far, so good. I think that most people who die in their pyjamas (a) either died in their sleep, which is a blessing, or (b) were with their family or in a hospital bed, meaning that death did not arrive suddenly, and they all had time to get used to 'the Unwanted Guest', as the Brazilian poet, Manuel Bandeira, called it.

The news item went on to say that, when he died, the man was in his bedroom. That cancels out the hospital hypothesis, leaving the possibility that he died in his sleep, without suffering, without even realizing that he wouldn't live to see the morning light again.

However, there remains one other possibility: that he was attacked and killed.

Anyone who knows Tokyo also knows that, although it is a vast city, it is also one of the safest places in the world. I remember once stopping with my Japanese publishers for a meal before driving on into the interior of Japan. All our cases were on the back seat of the car. I immediately said how dangerous this was; someone was bound to pass, see our luggage, and make off with our clothes and documents and everything else. My publisher smiled and told me not to worry; he had never known such a thing to happen in his entire life (and, indeed, nothing did happen to our luggage, although I spent the whole of supper feeling tense).

But let's go back to our dead man in pyjamas. There was no sign of struggle or violence. An official from the Metropolitan Police, in an interview with the newspaper, stated that the man had almost certainly died of a sudden heart attack. So we can also reject the murder hypothesis.

The corpse was found by the employees of a construction company on the second floor of a building in a housing development that was about to be demolished. Everything would lead us to think that our dead man in the pyjamas, having failed to find somewhere to live in one of the most densely populated and most expensive places in the world, had simply decided to live in a building where he wouldn't have to pay any rent.

Then comes the tragic part of the story. Our dead man was nothing more than a skeleton wearing pyjamas. Beside him, was an open newspaper dated 20 February 1984. On a table nearby, the calendar marked the same day.

He had been there for twenty years.

And no one had noticed his absence.

The man was identified as an ex-employee of the company who had built the housing development, where he had moved at the beginning of the 1980s, immediately after getting divorced. He was just over fifty on the day he was reading the newspaper and suddenly departed this life.

His ex-wife had never tried to get in touch with him. The journalists went to the company where he had worked and discovered that the company had gone bankrupt immediately after the project was finished, because they had failed to sell any of the apartments, which would explain why they did not find it strange when the man stopped turning up for work. The journalists tracked down his friends, who attributed his disappearance to the fact that he had borrowed money from them and hadn't been able to pay them back.

The news item ended by saying that the man's mortal remains were returned to his ex-wife. When I finished reading the article, I kept thinking about that final sentence: the ex-wife was still alive; and yet, for twenty years, she had never once tried to contact him. What can have been going on inside her mind? That he didn't love her any more, and that he had decided to cut her out of his life for good? That he had met another woman and disappeared? That this is simply what life is like once the divorce proceedings are over, and that there is no point in continuing a relationship once it has been legally terminated? I imagine what she must have felt when she learned the fate of the man with whom she had shared a large part of her life.

And then I thought about the dead man in pyjamas, about his complete and utter isolation, to the point that, for twenty long years, no one in the whole world had noticed that he had simply vanished without trace. I can only conclude that worse than hunger or thirst, worse than being unemployed, unhappy in love or defeated and in despair, far worse than any or all of those things, is feeling that no one, absolutely no one, cares about us.

Let us say a silent prayer for that man, and thank him for making us think about how important friends are.

The Solitary Piece of Coal

Juan always used to attend the Sunday service at his church, but he began to feel that the priest was always saying the same thing, and so stopped going.

Two months later, one cold winter night, the priest came to visit him.

'He's probably come to try and persuade me to go back,' Juan thought to himself. He felt that he couldn't give the real reason for his absence – the priest's repetitive sermons. He needed to find an excuse and, while he was thinking, he placed two chairs beside the fire and started talking about the weather.

The priest said nothing. After trying in vain for some time to start a conversation, Juan gave up. The two men sat on in silence for nearly half an hour, staring into the fire.

At that point, the priest got up and, with one of the logs that had not yet burned, he pushed one piece of coal away from the flames.

Since there was not enough heat for the coal to continue burning, it began to cool. Juan quickly drew it back into the centre of the fire.

'Good night,' said the priest, getting up to leave.

'Good night, and thank you very much,' replied Juan. 'However brightly a piece of coal may be burning, it will soon burn out if you remove it from the flames. However intelligent a man may be, he will soon lose his warmth and his flame if he distances himself from his fellow man. I'll see you at church next Sunday.'

Manuel Is an Important and Necessary Man

Manuel needs to be busy. If he is not, he thinks that his life has no meaning, that he's wasting his time, that society no longer needs him, that no one loves or wants him.

So, as soon as he wakes up, he has a series of tasks to perform: to watch the news on television (something might have happened in the night); to read the newspaper (something might have happened during the day yesterday); to tell his wife not to let the children be late for school; to take the car or catch a taxi or a bus or the metro, all the time thinking hard, staring into space, looking at his watch or, if possible, making a few calls on his mobile phone, and ensuring that everyone can see what an important man he is, useful to the world.

Manuel arrives at work and sits down to deal with the paperwork that awaits him. If he's an employee, he does his best to make sure that his boss has seen that he's arrived on time. If he's a boss, he sets everyone to work immediately. If there are no important tasks to be done, Manuel will invent them, create them, come up with a new plan, develop new lines of action.

Manuel goes to lunch, but never alone. If he is a boss, he sits down with his friends and discusses new strategies, speaks ill of his competitors, always has a card up his sleeve, complains (with some pride) of overwork. If Manuel is an employee, he, too, sits down with his friends, complains about his boss, complains about the amount of overtime he's doing, states with some anxiety (and with some pride) that various things in the company depend entirely on him.

Manuel – boss or employee – works all afternoon. From time to time, he looks at his watch. It's nearly time to go home, but he still has to sort out a detail here, sign a document there. He's an honest man and wants to justify his salary, other people's expectations, the dreams of his parents, who struggled so hard to give him a good education.

Finally, he goes home. He has a bath, puts on some more comfortable clothes, and has supper with his family. He asks after his children's homework and what his wife has been doing. Sometimes, he talks about his work, although only to serve as an example, because he tries not to bring his work problems home with him. They finish supper, and his children – who have no time for examples, homework, or other such things – immediately leave the table and go and sit down in front of the computer. Manuel, in turn, goes and sits down in front of that piece of apparatus from his childhood called the television. He again watches the news (something might have happened during the afternoon).

He always goes to bed with some technical book on his bedside table – whether he's a boss or an employee, he knows that competition is intense, and that anyone who fails to keep up to date runs the risk of losing his job and facing that worst of all curses: having nothing to do.

He talks a little to his wife; he is, after all, a nice, hard-working, loving man who takes care of his family, and is prepared to defend it whatever the circumstances. He falls asleep at once, and he sleeps knowing that he will be very busy tomorrow, and that he needs to rebuild his energies.

That night, Manuel has a dream. An angel asks him: 'Why are you doing this?' He replies that it's because he's a responsible man.

The angel goes on: 'Would you be capable of taking at least fifteen minutes of your day to stop and look at the world, and at yourself, and simply do nothing?' Manuel says that he would love to do that, but he doesn't have time. 'You're lying to me,' says the angel. 'Everyone has time to do that. It's just that they don't have the courage. Work is a blessing when it helps us to think about what we're doing; but it becomes a curse when its sole use is to stop us thinking about the meaning of our life.'

Manuel wakes up in the middle of the night in a cold sweat. Courage? How can a man who sacrifices himself for his family not have the courage to stop for fifteen minutes a day?

It's best to go back to sleep. It was just a dream; these questions will get him nowhere; and tomorrow he's going to be very, very busy.

Manuel Is a Free Man

M anuel works for thirty years without stopping. He brings up his children, sets a good example, and devotes all his time to work, never asking: 'Does what I'm doing have any meaning?' His one thought is that the busier he is, the more important he will be in the eyes of the world.

His children grow up and leave home. He gets promotion at work. One day, he receives a watch or a pen, as a reward for all those years of devotion. His friends shed a few tears, and the longed-for moment arrives: he's retired, free to do whatever he wants!

During the first few months, he occasionally visits the office where he worked, talks to his old friends, and surrenders to the pleasure of doing something he always dreamed of: getting up late. He goes for a walk along the beach or through town; he has his house in the country, earned by the sweat of his brow; he discovers gardening, and gradually penetrates the mysteries of plants and flowers. Manuel has time, all the time in the world. He travels, using some of the money he has managed to save. He visits museums and learns in two hours about ideas that took painters and sculptors from different eras centuries to develop; but he at least has the feeling that he is broadening his cultural knowledge. He takes hundreds and thousands of photos and sends them to his friends – after all, they need to know how happy he is.

More months pass. Manuel learns that the garden does not follow exactly the same rules as man – what he planted will take time to grow, and there is no point in constantly checking to see if there are buds on the rose bush yet. In a moment of genuine reflection, he discovers that all he saw on his journeys was the landscape outside the tourist bus, and monuments which are now preserved in various 6 x 9 photos. But the truth is, he did not feel any real excitement – he was more concerned with telling his friends about it than with actually experiencing the magic of being in a foreign country.

He continues to watch the television news and reads more newspapers (because he has more time), considering himself to be a very well-informed person, able to talk about things which, before, he had no time to study.

He looks for someone with whom to share his opinions, but they are all immersed in the river of life, working, doing something, envying Manuel his freedom and, at the same time, content to be useful to society, and to be 'occupied' with something important.

Manuel seeks comfort in his children. They always treat him with great affection – he has been an excellent father, an exemplar of honesty and dedication – but they, too, have other concerns, although they consider it their duty to be there for Sunday lunch.

Manuel is a free man, reasonably well off, well informed, with an impeccable past. But what now? What should he do with this hard-won freedom?

Everyone greets him and praises him, but no one has time for him. Gradually, Manuel begins to feel sad and useless, despite all those many years spent serving the world and his family.

One night, an angel appears to him while he sleeps: 'What have you done with your life? Did you try to live your life according to your dreams?'

Another long day begins. The newspapers. The TV news. The garden. Lunch. A short nap. He can do whatever he wants to do, except that, right now, he discovers, he doesn't want to do anything. Manuel is a sad, free man, just one step away from depression, because he was always too busy to think about the meaning of his life, and simply let the years flow under the bridge. He remembers the words of the poet: 'He passed through life/He did not live it'.

However, since it is too late to accept all this, it's best just to change the subject. His hard-won freedom is merely exile in disguise.

Manuel Goes to Paradise

For a while, Manuel enjoys the freedom of retirement, not having to get up at a particular time, and being able to use his time to do what he wants. However, he soon falls into depression. He feels useless, excluded from the society he helped to build, abandoned by his grown-up children, incapable of understanding the meaning of life, having never bothered to answer the old, old question: 'What am I doing here?'

Well, our dear, honest, dedicated Manuel finally dies – something that will happen to all the Manuels, Paulos, Marias, and Mônicas of this world. And here, I will let Henry Drummond, in his brilliant book, *The Greatest Thing in the World*, describe what happens next:

> Since earliest times people have asked the great question: What is the supreme good? You have life before you. You can only live it once. What is the noblest object of desire, the supreme gift to covet?
>
> We have been accustomed to be told that the greatest thing in the religious world is faith. That great word has been the keynote for centuries of the popular religion; and we have easily learned to look upon it as the greatest thing in the world. Well, we are wrong. If we have been told that, we may miss

the mark. In the 13th chapter of 1 Corinthians, Paul takes us to Christianity at its source, and there we see, 'The greatest of these is love.'

It is not an oversight. Paul was speaking of faith just a moment before. He says, 'And if I have all faith, so that I can remove mountains, and have not love, I am nothing.' So far from forgetting, he deliberately contrasts them, 'Now abideth faith, hope, love', and without a moment's hesitation the decision falls, 'The greatest of these is love.'

In this case, our Manuel is saved at the moment of his death because, despite never having given a meaning to his life, he was capable of loving, of providing for his family, and of doing his work in a dignified manner. Meanwhile, even though his life had a happy ending, his last days on earth were very complicated.

To use a phrase I heard Shimon Peres use at the World Economic Forum in Davos: 'The optimist and the pessimist both die in the end, but each lives his life in a completely different way.'

In Melbourne

This is to be my main appearance at the Writers' Festival in Melbourne, Australia. It is ten o'clock in the morning and there is a packed audience. I am to be interviewed by a local writer, John Felton.

I step onto the platform with my usual feelings of apprehension. Felton introduces me and starts asking me questions. Before I can finish what I'm saying, he interrupts me and asks me another question. When I reply, he says something like 'That wasn't a very clear answer.' Five minutes later, there is a feeling of unease amongst the audience; everyone can sense that something is wrong. I remember Confucius, and take the only possible action.

'Do you like what I write?' I ask.

'That's irrelevant,' Felton replies. 'I'm here to interview you, not the other way round.'

'But it is relevant. You won't let me finish my thought. Confucius says: "Whenever possible, be clear." Let's follow that advice and make things absolutely clear: Do you like what I write?'

'No, I don't. I've read two of your books, and I hated both of them.'

'Fine, now we can continue.'

The lines of battle have been drawn. The audience relaxes, and the atmosphere becomes electric; the interview becomes a real debate, and everyone – including Felton – is pleased with the result.

The Pianist in the Shopping Mall

I am wandering distractedly through a shopping mall with my violinist friend, Ursula, who was born in Hungary and is now a leading figure in two international orchestras. Suddenly, she grips my arm:

'Listen!'

I listen. I hear the voices of adults, a child screaming, the noise from televisions in the shops selling electrical appliances, high heels clicking over the tiled floor, and the inevitable music that is played in every shopping mall in the world.

'Isn't it wonderful?'

I say that I can't hear anything wonderful or unusual.

'The piano!' she says, looking at me with an air of disappointment. 'The pianist is marvellous!'

'It must be a recording.'

'Don't be silly.'

When I listen more intently, it is clear that the music is, indeed, live. The person is playing a sonata by Chopin, and now that I can concentrate, the notes seem to hide all the other sounds surrounding us. We walk along the walkways crowded with people, shops, bargains, and with things which, according to the announcements, everyone has, except me and you. We reach the food hall, where people are eating, talking, arguing, reading newspapers, and where there is one of those special attractions that all malls try to offer their customers.

In this case, it is a piano and a pianist.

The pianist plays two more Chopin sonatas, then pieces by Schubert and Mozart. He must be around thirty. A notice beside the stage explains that he is a famous musician from Georgia, one of the ex-Soviet republics. He must have looked for work, found all doors closed, despaired, given up, and now here he is in this mall.

Except that I'm not sure he is really here: his eyes are fixed on the magical world where the music was composed; his hands share with us all his love, his soul, his enthusiasm, the very best of himself, all his years of study, concentration and discipline.

The one thing he appears not to have understood is that no one, absolutely no one, has gone there to listen to him; they have gone there to buy, to eat, to pass the time, to window-shop, or to meet friends. A couple of people stop beside us, talking loudly, and then move on. The pianist does not notice – he is still conversing with Mozart's angels. Nor has he noticed that he has an audience of two, one of whom is an extremely gifted violinist and is listening with tears in her eyes.

I remember going into a chapel once and seeing a young woman playing for God, but that was in a chapel and made some kind of sense. Here, though, no one is listening, possibly not even God.

That's a lie. God is listening. God is in the soul, and in the hands of this man, because he is giving the very best of himself, regardless of whether or not he is noticed, regardless of the money he gets paid. He is playing as if he were at the Scala in Milan or the Opéra in Paris. He is playing because that is his fate, his joy, his reason for living.

I am filled by a profound sense of reverence and respect for a man who is, at that moment, reminding me of a very important lesson: that we each of us have our personal legend to fulfil, and that is all. It doesn't matter if other people support us or criticize us, or ignore us, or put up with us – we are doing it because that is our destiny on this earth, and the fount of all joy.

The pianist ends with another piece by Mozart and, for the first time, he notices our presence. He gives us a discreet, polite nod, and we do the same. Then he returns to his paradise, and it is best to leave him there, untouched by the world, or even by our timid applause. He is serving as an example to us. Whenever we feel that no one is paying any attention to what we are doing, let us think of that pianist. He was talking to God through his work, and nothing else mattered.

On My Way to the Chicago Book Fair

I was flying from New York to Chicago to attend the book fair held by the American Booksellers Association. Suddenly, a young man stood up in the aisle of the plane and announced:

'I need twelve volunteers each willing to carry a single rose when we get off the plane.'

Several people raised their hands. I did too, but wasn't chosen.

Even so, I decided to follow the group. We landed, and the young man indicated a young woman in the arrivals hall at O'Hare Airport. One by one, the passengers presented their roses to her. At last, in front of everyone, the young man asked her to marry him, and she accepted.

An air steward said to me:

'I've been working here for years, and that's the most romantic thing that has ever happened in this airport.'

Of Poles and Rules

In the autumn of 2003, I was strolling through the centre of Stockholm late one night when I saw a woman walking along using ski poles. My first reaction was to assume that she must have had an accident, but then I noticed that she was moving swiftly and rhythmically, just as if she were skiing, except, of course, that we were surrounded by asphalt. The obvious conclusion was: 'The woman must be mad. How can she possibly pretend she's skiing in a city?'

Back at the hotel, I mentioned it to my publisher. He said that if anyone was mad it was me. What I had seen was a form of exercise known as Nordic walking. According to him, it gave you a much more comprehensive workout because, as well as moving your legs, your arms, shoulders and back muscles were also used.

When I go walking (which, along with archery, is my favourite pastime), my intention is to be able to reflect and think, to look at the marvellous things around me, and to talk to my wife as we walk. I found what my publisher said very interesting, but I thought no more about it.

One day, I was in a sports shop, buying some archery equipment, when I saw some new poles for mountaineers. They were made of light aluminium and could be made shorter or longer like a telescopic photographic tripod. I remembered the Nordic walking – why not try it? I bought two pairs, one for me, and one for my wife. We adjusted the poles to a comfortable height and decided to use them the following day.

It was an amazing discovery! We walked up a mountain and back down again, and we really did feel as if our whole body was moving, plus our balance was better and we got less tired. We walked twice the distance we usually cover in an hour. I remembered wanting to explore the dried-up bed of a stream, but having to give up because of the difficulties I had in walking over the stones. With the poles, I thought, it would be much easier, and I was right.

My wife went on the internet and found that she was burning 46 per cent more calories than when doing normal walking. She got really excited about it, and Nordic walking became part of our daily lives.

One evening, just for amusement, I decided to see what else I could find out about it on the internet. I had a real shock. There were pages and pages, with federations, groups, discussions, models, and … rules.

I don't know what made me open the page on rules; but as I read it, I grew increasingly dismayed. I was doing everything wrong! My poles should be adjusted to a longer length; I should be keeping to a certain rhythm and holding the pole at a particular angle; there was some very complicated movement of the shoulder, and a different way of using your elbow. In short, everything had to conform to certain rigid, prescriptive techniques.

I printed out all the pages. The next day – and the days that followed – I tried to do exactly what the experts were telling me to do. The walk became less interesting; I stopped noticing all the marvels around me, and hardly spoke to my wife at all – the only thing I could think about were the rules. After a week, I asked myself: why am I learning all this?

My aim was not to do some sort of keep-fit exercise. I am sure that the people who started doing Nordic walking in the first place were merely thinking of the pleasure of walking, of improving their balance and moving their whole body. We knew intuitively what was the best length of pole for us, just as we could intuitively deduce that the closer we held the poles to our body, the better and easier the movement. But now, because of those rules, I had stopped concentrating on the things I loved and was more concerned about burning calories, moving my muscles, and using a particular part of my spine.

I decided to forget everything I had learned. Now we go walking with our poles, enjoying the world around us, and feeling our bodies being worked, moved and balanced. If I wanted to do a keep-fit workout rather than a kind of walking meditation, I would go to a gym. For the moment, I am happy with my relaxed, instinctive Nordic walking, even if I'm not burning off that 46 per cent of extra calories.

I don't know why we human beings are so obsessed with making rules about everything.

The Piece of Bread That Fell Wrong Side Up

We all have a tendency to believe in 'Murphy's Law': that everything we do will turn out wrong. Jean Claude Carrière has an interesting story about precisely that feeling.

A man was quietly eating his breakfast. Suddenly, the piece of bread that he had just spread with butter fell to the ground.

Imagine his surprise when he looked down and saw that it had landed buttered side up! The man thought he had witnessed a miracle. Excited, he went to tell his friends what had happened, and they were all amazed; because when a piece of bread falls on the floor, it nearly always lands buttered side down, making a mess of everything.

'Perhaps you're a saint,' one friend said. 'And this is a sign from God.'

Soon the whole village knew, and they all started animatedly discussing the incident: how was it that, against all expectations, the man's slice of bread had fallen on the floor buttered side up? Since no one could come up with a credible answer, they went to see a Teacher, who lived nearby and told him the story.

The Teacher requested that he be given one night to pray, reflect, and seek divine inspiration. The following day, they all returned, eager for an answer.

'It's quite simple really,' said the Teacher. 'The fact is, that the piece of bread fell exactly as it should have fallen, but the butter had been spread on the wrong side.'

Of Books and Libraries

I don't really own many books. A few years ago, driven by the idea of getting the maximum quality of life with the minimum number of possessions, I made certain choices. This doesn't mean that I opted for the life of a monk; on the contrary, divesting yourself of many of your possessions gives you enormous freedom. Some of my friends (male and female) complain that, because they have so many clothes, they waste hours of their life trying to decide what to wear. Now that I have reduced my wardrobe to 'basic black', I no longer have this problem.

However, I'm not here to talk about fashion, but about books. To return to my main point, I decided to keep only four hundred books in my library, some because they have sentimental value, others because I'm always re-reading them. I took this decision for various reasons, and one of them was the sadness I felt at seeing how libraries, which have been painstakingly acquired over a lifetime, are often simply sold off as a job lot once the collector is dead, with no respect shown for them at all. Also why keep all these books at home? To prove to my friends how cultivated I am? To decorate the walls? The books I have bought would be of far more use in a public library than in my house.

I used to say that I needed my books in case I ever wanted to look something up in them. Now, however, when I want to find out something, I turn on my computer, type in the key word or words, and everything I need to know appears on the screen – courtesy of the internet, the biggest library on the planet.

Of course, I still continue to buy books – there's no electronic substitute for them; but as soon as I've finished a book, I let it go; I give it to someone else, or to the public library. My intention is not to save forests or to be generous. I simply believe that a book has its own journey to make, and should not be condemned to being stuck on a shelf.

Being a writer and living, as I do, on royalties, I might be working to my own detriment; after all, the more books that are bought, the more money I earn. However, that would be unfair on the reader, especially in countries where a large part of the government budget for buying books for libraries is clearly not based on the two main criteria for making a serious choice – the pleasure one gets from reading a book, plus the quality of the writing.

Let's leave our books free to travel, then, to be touched by other hands, and enjoyed by other eyes. As I'm writing this, I have a vague memory of a poem by Jorge Luis Borges, which speaks of books that will never again be opened.

Where am I now? Sitting in a café in a small Pyrenean town in France, enjoying the air-conditioning, because the heat outside is unbearable. I happen to have Borges' complete works in my house, which is a few kilometres from where I'm writing this – he's one of those authors I constantly read and re-read. But why not put my theory to the test?

I cross the street and make the five-minute walk to another café, one that is equipped with computers (an establishment known by the nice, but contradictory, name of 'cyber-café'). I greet the owner, order a glass of ice-cold mineral water, go to a search engine, and key in some of the words of the one line I do remember, along with the name of the author. In less than two minutes, I have the poem before me:

> *There is a line from Verlaine I'll never now recall,*
> *There is a street nearby from which my footsteps are barred,*
> *There is a mirror that has looked its last on my face,*
> *There is a door I have closed for the final time.*
> *Amongst the books in my library (I can see them now)*
> *There are some I will never open again.*

I felt exactly the same about many of the books I gave away: that I would simply never open them again, because new, interesting books are constantly being published, and I love to read. Now, I think it's wonderful that people should have libraries; generally speaking, a child's first contact with books arises out of their curiosity to find out about those bound volumes containing pictures and words; but I find it equally wonderful when, at a book-signing, a reader comes up to me clutching a battered copy of one of my books that has been passed from friend to friend dozens of times. This means that the book has travelled just as its author's mind travelled while he was writing it.

Prague, 1981

Once, in the winter of 1981, I was walking with my wife through the streets of Prague and we came across a young man making drawings of the buildings around him.

Although I have a real horror of carrying things when I'm travelling (and we still had a lot of journeying ahead of us), I really liked one of the drawings and decided to buy it.

When I held out the money, I noticed that the young man was not wearing gloves, despite the –5°C temperatures.

'Why aren't you wearing gloves?' I asked.

'So that I can hold my pencil.'

And he began telling me how he adored Prague in winter, and how it was the best season in which to draw the city. He was so pleased with this sale, that he asked if he could draw a portrait of my wife – without charge.

While I was waiting for him to finish the drawing, I realized that something strange had happened. We had been talking for almost five minutes, and yet neither of us could speak the other's language. We made ourselves understood by gestures, smiles, facial expressions, and the desire to share something.

That simple desire to share something meant that we could enter the world of language without words, where everything is always clear, and there is no danger of being misinterpreted.

For the Woman Who Is All Women

A week after the 2003 Frankfurt Book Fair, I get a call from my Norwegian publisher. The organizers of the concert being arranged for the winner of the Nobel Peace Prize, Shirin Ebadi, would like me to write something for the event.

This is an honour I should not refuse; after all, Shirin Ebadi is a legendary figure. She may be less than five feet tall, but she has sufficient stature to speak out in defence of human rights, and to have her voice heard all around the world. At the same time, I feel slightly nervous about such a responsibility – the event will be televised in 110 countries, and I have only two minutes to talk about someone who has dedicated her whole life to other people. I walk in the forests near the old mill where I live when I am in Europe. Several times, I consider phoning to tell them that I can't think of anything to say; but then, what makes life interesting are the challenges we face, and so I end up accepting the invitation.

I travel to Oslo on 9 December, and the following day – a lovely, sunny day – I am in the audience at the award ceremony. The vast windows of the Prefecture provide a view of the port where, at about the same time of year, twenty years before, I had sat with my wife, looking out at the icy sea and eating prawns that had just been brought in by the fishing boats. I think of the long journey that has brought me from that port to this room, but my memories of the past are interrupted by the sound of trumpets and the arrival of the Queen and the royal family. The organizing committee hands over the prize, and Shirin Ebadi gives a passionate speech denouncing the way certain governments are using the so-called war on terror as a justification for trying to create a kind of worldwide police state.

That night, at the concert in honour of the prizewinner, Catherine Zeta-Jones announces that my text will be read. At that moment, I press a button on my mobile phone, and the phone rings in the old mill where I live (this has all been planned beforehand), and my wife is suddenly there with me, listening to Michael Douglas as he reads my words.

This is what I wrote, words which can, I think, be applied to all those who are working to create a better world.

The Persian poet Rumi once said that life is like being sent by a king to another country in order to carry out a particular task. The person sent may do a hundred other things in that other country, but if he or she fails to fulfil the particular task he or she was charged with, it is as if nothing had been done.

To the woman who understood her task.

To the woman who looked at the road ahead of her, and knew that hers would be a difficult journey.

To the woman who did not attempt to make light of those difficulties, but, on the contrary, spoke out against them and made them clearly visible.

To the woman who made the lonely feel less alone, who fed those who hungered and thirsted for justice, who made the oppressor feel as bad as those he oppressed.

To the woman who always keeps her door open, her hands working, her feet moving.

To the woman who personifies the verses of that other Persian poet, Hafez, when he says:

Not even seven thousand years of joy can justify seven days of repression.

To the woman who is here tonight, may she be each and every one of us, may her example spread, may she still have many difficult days ahead, so that she can complete her work, so that, for the generations to come, the meaning of 'injustice' will be found only in dictionary definitions and never in the lives of human beings.

And may she travel slowly, because her pace is the pace of change, and change, real change, always takes a very long time.

A Visitor Arrives From Morocco

A visitor arrives from Morocco and tells me a curious story about how certain desert tribes perceive original sin.

Eve was walking in the Garden of Eden when the serpent slithered over to her.

'Eat this apple,' said the serpent.

Eve, who had been properly instructed by God, refused.

'Eat this apple,' insisted the serpent. 'You need to look more beautiful for your man.'

'No, I don't,' replied Eve. 'He has no other woman but me.'

The serpent laughed.

'Of course he has.'

And when Eve did not believe him, he led her up to a well on the top of a hill.

'She's in that cave. Adam hid her in there.'

Eve leaned over and, reflected in the water of the well, she saw a lovely woman. She immediately ate the apple the serpent was holding out to her.

According to this same Moroccan tribe, a return to paradise is guaranteed to anyone who recognizes his or her reflection in the water and feels no fear.

My Funeral

The journalist from *The Mail on Sunday* appears at my hotel in London and asks one simple question: 'If you were to die today, what kind of funeral would you like?'

The truth is that the idea of death has been with me every day since 1986, when I walked the Road to Santiago. Up until then, I had always been terrified at the thought that, one day, everything would end; but on one of the stages of that pilgrimage, I performed an exercise that consisted in experiencing what it felt like to be buried alive. It was such an intense experience that I lost all fear, and afterwards saw death as my daily companion, who is always by my side, saying: 'I will touch you, but you don't know when. Therefore live life as intensely as you can.'

Because of this, I never leave until tomorrow what I can do or experience today – and that includes joys, work obligations, saying I'm sorry if I feel I've offended someone, and contemplation of the present moment as if it were my last. I can remember many occasions when I have smelled the perfume of death: that far-off day in 1974, in Aterro do Flamengo (Rio de Janeiro), when the taxi I was travelling in was blocked by another car, and a group of armed paramilitaries jumped out and put a hood over my head. Even though they assured me that nothing bad would happen to me, I was convinced that I was about to become another of the military regime's 'disappeared'.

Or when, in August 1989, I got lost on a climb in the Pyrenees. I looked around at the mountains bare of snow and vegetation, thought that I wouldn't have the strength to go back, and concluded that my body would not be found until the following summer. Finally, after wandering around for many hours, I managed to find a track that led me to a remote village.

The journalist from *The Mail on Sunday* insists: but what would my funeral be like? Well, according to my will, there will be no funeral. I have decided to be cremated, and my wife will scatter my ashes in a place called El Cebrero in Spain – the place where I found my sword. Any unpublished manuscripts and typescripts will remain unpublished (I'm horrified at the number of 'posthumous works' or 'trunks full of papers' that writers' heirs unscrupulously publish in order to make some money; if the authors chose not to publish these things while they were alive, their privacy should be respected). The sword that I found on the Road to Santiago will be thrown into the sea, and thus be returned to the place whence it came. And my money, along with the royalties that will continue to be received for another seventy years, will be devoted entirely to the charitable foundation I have set up.

'And what about your epitaph?' asks the journalist. Well, since I'm going to be cremated, there won't be a headstone on which to write an inscription, since my ashes will have been carried away on the wind. But if I had to choose a phrase, I would choose this: 'He died while he was still alive.' That might seem a contradiction in terms; but I know a lot of people who have stopped living, even though they continue working and eating and carrying on with their usual social activities. They do everything on automatic pilot, unaware of the magic moment that each day brings with it, never stopping to think about the miracle of life, not understanding that the next minute could be their last on the face of this planet.

The journalist leaves, and I sit down at the computer and decide to write this. I know it's not a topic anyone likes to think about, but I have a duty to my readers – to make them think about the important things in life. And death is possibly *the* most important thing. We are all walking towards death, but we never know when death will touch us and it is our duty, therefore, to look around us, to be grateful for each minute. But we should also be grateful to death, because it makes us think about the importance of each decision we take, or fail to take; it makes us stop doing anything that keeps us stuck in the category of the 'living dead' and, instead, urges us to risk everything, to bet everything on those things we always dreamed of doing, because, whether we like it or not, the angel of death is waiting for us.

Restoring the Web

In New York, I meet up for afternoon tea with a rather unusual artist. She works in a bank in Wall Street, but one day she had a dream, in which she was told to visit twelve different places in the world and, in each one of those places, to create a painting or a sculpture in Nature itself.

So far, she has managed to make four such works. She shows me photos of one of them – a carving of an Indian inside a cave in California. While she waits for further signs to be revealed to her in dreams, she continues working at the bank, and that way earns enough money to travel and to carry out her task.

I ask her why she does it.

'In order to maintain the equilibrium of the world,' she replies. 'It may sound like nonsense, but there is a tenuous web around us all, which we can make stronger or weaker depending on how we behave. We can save or destroy many things with a simple gesture that might, at times, seem utterly pointless. My dreams may be nonsense too, but I don't want to run the risk of not following them. For me, human relationships are like a vast, fragile spider's web. What I'm trying to do with my work is to restore part of that web.'

These Are My Friends

The reason the king is so powerful is because he's made a pact with the Devil,' a very devout woman in the street told the boy, and he was intrigued.

Some time later, when he was travelling to another town, the boy heard a man beside him remark:

'All this land belongs to the same man. I'd say the Devil had a hand in that.'

Late one summer afternoon, a beautiful woman walked past the boy.

'That woman is in the service of Satan!' cried a preacher angrily.

From then on, the boy decided to seek the Devil out, and when he found him, he said:

'They say you can make people powerful, rich, and beautiful.'

'Not really,' replied the Devil. 'You've just been listening to the views of those who are trying to promote me.'

How Do We Survive?

I receive through the post three litres of a product intended to provide a substitute for milk. A Norwegian company wants to know if I'm interested in investing in the production of this new kind of food because, in the opinion of the expert David Rietz: 'ALL [his capitals] cow's milk contains 59 active hormones, a great deal of fat, cholesterol, dioxins, bacteria and viruses.'

I think of the calcium that, when I was a child, my mother said was so good for my bones; but the expert is ahead of me: 'Calcium? Where do cows get calcium for their big bones? Yes, from plants!' Naturally, this new product is plant-based, and milk is condemned on the basis of innumerable studies carried out by various institutes dotted around the world.

And protein? David Rietz is implacable: 'Milk can be thought of as "liquid meat" [I never have, but he must know what he's talking about] because of its high protein content. But it is the protein which may actually leach calcium from the body. Countries that consume high protein diets also have the highest rates of osteoporosis.'

That same afternoon, my wife e-mails me an article she has found on the internet:

People who are now aged between 40 and 60 years old used to drive around in cars with no seatbelts, no head support and no airbag. Children sat in the back, making a tremendous racket and having a great time.

Baby cribs were painted with brightly coloured paints, all highly suspect, since they might have contained lead or some other dangerous substance.

I, for example, am of the generation that used to make their own 'go-karts' (I don't know quite how to explain this to today's generation – let's just say they were made with ball bearings fixed inside two iron hoops) and we would race down the hills in Botafogo, using our feet as brakes, falling off, hurting ourselves, but very proud of our high-speed adventures.

The article continues:

There were no mobile phones, and so our parents had no way of knowing where we were – how was that possible? As children, we were never right, we were occasionally punished, but we never had any psychological problems about feeling rejected or unloved. At school, there were good pupils and there were bad pupils: the good pupils moved up to the next year, the bad ones flunked. Psychotherapists were not called in to study the case – the bad pupils simply had to repeat the year.

And even so, we managed to survive with a few grazed knees and a few traumas. We not only survived, we look back nostalgically to the days when milk was not a poison, when a child was expected to resolve any problems without outside help, getting into fights if necessary, and spending much of the day without any electronic toys, and, instead, inventing games with friends.

But let's go back to my initial topic. I decided to try the miraculous new product that could replace murderous milk.

I got no further than the first mouthful.

I asked my wife and my maid to try it, without telling them what it was. They both said they had never tasted anything so disgusting in their life.

I'm worried about tomorrow's children, with their computer games, their parents with mobile phones, psychotherapists helping them through every failure, and – above all – being forced to drink this 'magic potion', which will keep them free of cholesterol, osteoporosis, and safe from those 59 active hormones and from toxins.

They will be very healthy and well balanced; and when they grow up, they will discover milk (by then, it may well be illegal). Perhaps some scientist in 2050 will take it upon himself to rescue something that people have been drinking since the beginning of time? Or will milk only be available from drug traffickers?

Marked Out to Die

I possibly should have died at 22:30 on 22 August 2004, less than forty-eight hours after my birthday. In order for the scene of my near-death to be set, a series of factors came into play:

(a) In interviews to promote his latest film, the actor Will Smith kept mentioning my book *The Alchemist*.

(b) His latest film was based on a book I had read years ago and very much enjoyed: *I, Robot*. I decided to go and see it, in homage to Smith and Asimov.

(c) The film opened in a small town in the south-west of France in the first week of August. However, for a series of entirely trivial reasons, I had to postpone going to the cinema until that Sunday.

I ate supper early and drank half a bottle of wine with my wife. We invited our maid to come with us (she resisted at first, but finally accepted); we got there in plenty of time, bought some popcorn, saw the film, and enjoyed it.

I got into the car to make the ten-minute drive back to the old converted mill that is my home. I put a CD of Brazilian music on and decided to drive fairly slowly so that, during those ten minutes, I could listen to at least three songs.

On the road, passing through small, sleepy villages, I see – appearing out of nowhere – a pair of headlights in the driver's side mirror. Before us lies a crossroads, clearly marked by posts.

I try to brake, because I know that the other car won't be able to overtake – the posts at the crossroads make that impossible. All this takes a fraction of a second. I remember thinking, 'The guy must be mad!', but I don't have time to say anything. The driver of the other car (the image engraved on my memory is that of a Mercedes, but I can't be sure), sees the posts, accelerates, pulls over in front of me, and when he tries to correct his position, ends up slewed across the road.

From then on, everything seems to happen in slow-motion. His car turns over on its side once, twice, three times. It hits the hard shoulder and continues rolling over and over, forward this time, with the front and back bumpers hitting the ground.

My headlights illuminate the whole thing, but I can't brake suddenly – I'm driving right alongside this car performing somersaults. It's like a scene from the film I've just seen; but that was fiction, and this is real life!

The car returns to the road and finally stops, lying on its left side. I can see the driver's shirt. I stop beside him with just one thought in my head: I must get out and help him. At that moment, I feel my wife's nails digging into my arm: she is begging me, please, to drive on and park further off; the other car might explode, catch fire.

I drive on for another hundred metres and park. The CD continues playing the Brazilian music as if nothing had happened. Everything seems so surreal, so distant. My wife and Isabel, the maid, run towards the scene of

the accident. Another car, coming in the opposite direction, stops. A woman jumps out, looking very upset.
Her headlights, too, have lit up that Dantesque scene.
She asks if I've got a mobile phone. I do. Then why
don't I phone for an ambulance!

What is the emergency number? She looks at me –
everyone knows that! 51 51 51! My mobile phone is
switched off – at the cinema, they always remind
patrons to do that. I key in the access code and we
phone the emergency number – 51 51 51. I know exactly where it all happened: between the villages of
Laloubère and Horgues.

My wife and the maid return: the boy in the car has
a few scratches, but apparently nothing very grave.
Nothing very grave, after what I saw, after turning over
six times! He staggers slightly when he gets out of the
car; other motorists stop; the firemen are on the scene
within five minutes; everything is all right.

Everything is all right. But he had been a fraction of
a second away from hitting our car and hurling us into
the ditch; things, then, would have been very bad for
all of us. Very bad indeed.

When I get home, I look up at the stars. Sometimes
we encounter things on our path, but because our time
has not yet come, they brush past us, without touching
us, even though they were close enough for us to see
them. I thank God for the awareness to understand, as
a friend of mine says, that everything that had to happen happened, but nothing did.

The Moment of Dawn

During the World Economic Forum at Davos, the winner of the Nobel Prize for Peace, Shimon Peres, told the following story.

A Rabbi gathered together his students and asked them:

'How do we know the exact moment when night ends and day begins?'

'When it's light enough to tell a sheep from a dog,' said one boy.

Another student said: 'No, when it's light enough to tell an olive tree from a fig tree.'

'No, that's not a good definition either.'

'Well, what's the right answer?' asked the boys.

And the Rabbi said:

'When a stranger approaches, and we think he is our brother, and all conflicts disappear, that is the moment when night ends and day begins.'

A January Day in 2005

It's raining hard today, and the temperature is about 3°C. I decide to go for a walk – I don't feel that I work properly if I don't walk every day – but it's very windy too, and so, after about ten minutes, I drive back home. I pick up the newspaper from my mailbox, but it contains nothing of importance, only the things that journalists have decided we should know, feel involved in, and have an opinion about.

I go over to my computer to check my e-mails.

Nothing new, just a few unimportant decisions to be made which take me no time at all to resolve.

I try doing some archery, but the wind makes it impossible. I've written my latest biennial book, which, this time, is entitled *The Zahir* and which won't be published for several weeks. I've written the columns I publish on the internet. I've updated my web page. I've had my stomach checked out and, fortunately, no abnormality was found (I had been very frightened about having a tube put down my throat, but it turned out to be nothing very terrible). I've been to the dentist. The plane tickets I'd been waiting for have finally arrived by express mail. I have things to do tomorrow and things which I finished yesterday, but today …

Today I have absolutely nothing that requires my attention.

I feel uneasy. Shouldn't I be doing something? Well, if I wanted to invent work, that wouldn't take much effort. We all have projects to develop, light bulbs to change, leaves to sweep, books to put away, computer files to organize. But how about just facing up to the void?

I put on a hat, thermal clothes, and a waterproof jacket and go out into the garden. That way, I should be able to withstand the cold for the next four or five hours. I sit down on the wet grass and start making a mental list of what is going through my head:

(a) I'm useless. Everyone else at that moment is busy, working hard.

Answer: I work hard too, sometimes twelve hours a day. Today I just happen to have nothing to do.

(b) I have no friends. Here I am, one of the most famous writers in the world, and I'm all alone; even the phone doesn't ring.

Answer: Of course I have friends, but they respect my need for solitude when I'm at the old mill in St Martin in France.

(c) I need to go and buy some glue.

Yes, I've just remembered that yesterday I ran out of glue. Why not jump in the car and go to the nearest town? And I stop at that thought. Why is it so difficult to stay as I am now, doing nothing?

A series of thoughts cross my mind: friends who worry about things that haven't yet happened; acquaintances who manage to fill every minute of their lives with tasks that seem to me absurd; senseless conversations; long telephone calls in which nothing of any importance is ever said; bosses who invent work in order to justify their jobs; officials who feel afraid because they have been given nothing important to do that day, which might mean that they are no longer useful; mothers who torment themselves because their children have gone out for the evening; students who torment themselves over their studies, over tests and exams.

I have a long, hard struggle with myself not to get up and go to the stationery shop to buy that glue. I experience terrible feelings of anxiety, but I am determined to stay here doing nothing, at least for a few hours. Gradually, the anxiety gives way to contemplation, and I start to listen to my soul. It has been longing to speak to me, but I'm always too busy.

The wind is still blowing very hard, and I know that it's cold and rainy, and that tomorrow I might perhaps need to buy some glue. I'm not doing anything, and yet I'm also doing the most important thing a man can do: I'm listening to what I needed to hear from myself.

A Man Lying on the Ground

On 1 July 1997, at five past one in the afternoon, there was a man of about fifty lying on the sea front in Copacabana. I glanced down at him as I walked by; then I continued on to the stall where I usually go for a drink of coconut water.

As a resident of Rio de Janeiro, I must have passed by such men, women, or children hundreds or even thousands of times. As someone who has travelled widely, I have seen the same scene in almost every country I have visited, from wealthy Sweden to impoverished Romania. I have seen people lying on the ground in all weathers: in the icy winters of Madrid or Paris or New York, where they stay close to the hot air vents outside the subway stations; in the scalding Lebanese sun, amongst the rubble of buildings destroyed by years of war. People lying on the ground – drunk, homeless, tired – are not a novelty to anyone.

I drank my coconut water. I needed to get home quickly because I had an interview with Juan Arias from the Spanish newspaper *El País*. On the way back, I noticed that the man was still there, lying in the sun, and everyone who passed did exactly the same as I had: glanced at him and then moved on.

Although I didn't know it, my soul was weary of seeing the same scene over and over. When I passed the man again, something stronger than myself made me kneel down and try to lift him up.

He did not respond. I turned his head and noticed blood on his temple. What now? Was it a bad wound? I dabbed at his skin with my T-shirt; it didn't look like anything serious.

At that moment, the man began muttering something about 'make them stop hitting me'. So he was alive; now what I needed to do was to get him out of the sun and to call the police.

I stopped the first man who passed and asked him to help me drag the injured man over to the shade between the sea front and the beach. The passer-by was wearing a suit and carrying a briefcase and various packages, but he put these down to help me – his soul was weary of seeing that same scene too.

Once we had placed the man in the shade, I headed off to my house. I knew there was a Military Police post nearby where I could ask for help. But before I got there, I met two policemen.

'There's a man who's been beaten up opposite number so-and-so,' I said. 'I've laid him down on the sand. It would be a good idea to call an ambulance.'

The two policemen said they would take steps. Right, I had done my duty. A boy scout is always prepared. My good deed for the day. The problem was in other hands now; it was up to them to deal with it. And the Spanish journalist would be arriving at my house at any moment.

I had not gone ten steps, when a stranger stopped me. In garbled Portuguese he said:

'I've already told the police about the man. They said that since he's not a thief, he's not their problem.'

I did not let the man finish. I walked back to where the policemen were standing, convinced that they would know who I was, that I wrote for the newspapers, that I appeared on television. I did so under the false impression that, sometimes, success can help to resolve matters.

'Are you some kind of official?' one of them asked when I became more insistent in my request for help.

They had no idea who I was.

'No, but we're going to resolve this problem right now.'

There I was, all sweaty and dressed in a blood-stained T-shirt and a pair of Bermuda shorts made from some old cut-down jeans. I was just an ordinary, anonymous man with no authority apart from my own weariness with all those years of seeing people lying on the ground and never doing anything about it.

And that changed everything. There are moments when you are suddenly free from any inhibitions or fears. There are moments when your eyes have a different light, and people know that you are absolutely serious. The policemen went with me and called an ambulance.

On my way back home, I went over the three lessons I had learned from that walk. (a) Anyone can abandon an action when it's still at the 'romantic' stage. (b) There is always someone to tell you: 'Now that you've started, finish.' And (c) everyone has the authority of an official when he or she is absolutely convinced of what he or she is doing.

The Missing Brick

Once, when I and my wife were travelling, I received a fax from my secretary.

'There's one glass brick missing for the work on the kitchen renovation,' she said. 'I'm sending you the original plan as well as the plan the builder has come up with to compensate for it.'

On the one hand, there was the design my wife had made: harmonious lines of bricks with an opening for ventilation. On the other, there was the plan drawn up to resolve the problem of the missing brick: a real jigsaw puzzle in which the glass squares were arranged in a higgledy-piggledy fashion that defied aesthetics.

'Just buy another brick,' wrote my wife. And so they did, and thus stuck to the original design.

That afternoon, I thought for a long time about what had happened; how often, for the lack of one brick, we completely distort the original plan of our lives.

Raj Tells Me a Story

A widow from a poor village in Bengal did not have enough money to pay for her son's bus fare, and so, when the boy started going to school, he would have to walk through the forest all on his own. In order to reassure him, she said:

'Don't be afraid of the forest, my son. Ask your God Krishna to go with you. He will hear your prayer.'

The boy followed his mother's suggestion; Krishna duly appeared; and from then on, accompanied him to school every day.

When it was his teacher's birthday, the boy asked his mother for some money in order to buy him a present.

'We haven't any money, son. Ask your brother Krishna to get you a present.'

The following day, the boy explained his problem to Krishna, who gave him a jug of milk.

The boy proudly handed the milk to the teacher, but the other boys' presents were far superior and the teacher didn't even notice his gift.

'Take that jug of milk to the kitchen,' said the teacher to an assistant.

The assistant did as he was told. However, when he tried to empty the jug, he found that it immediately filled up again of its own accord. He informed the teacher, who was amazed and asked the boy:

'Where did you get that jug, and how does it manage to stay full all the time?'

'Krishna, the god of the forest, gave it to me.'

The teacher, the students and the assistant all burst out laughing.

'There are no gods in the forest. That's pure superstition,' said the teacher. 'If he exists, let's all go and see him.'

The whole group set off. The boy started calling for Krishna, but he did not appear. The boy made one last desperate appeal.

'Brother Krishna, my teacher wants to see you. Please show yourself!'

At that moment, a voice emerged and echoed throughout the forest.

'How can he possibly want to see me, my son? He doesn't even believe I exist!'

The Other Side of the Tower of Babel

I have spent the whole morning explaining that I'm more interested in the country's inhabitants than in museums and churches, and that it would, therefore, be much better if we went to the market. They tell me that today is a national holiday and the market is closed.

'Where are we going then?'

'To a church.'

I knew it.

'Today we are celebrating a saint who is very special to us, and doubtless to you too. We are going to visit the tomb of this saint. But don't ask any questions and accept that sometimes we lay on some very nice surprises for our writers.'

'How long will it take to get there?'

'Twenty minutes.'

Twenty minutes is the standard answer. I know, of course, that it will take much longer than that. However, they have, up until now, respected all my wishes, so I had better give in on this one.

On this Sunday morning, I am in Yerevan, in Armenia. I reluctantly get into the car. I can see snow-covered Mount Ararat in the distance. I look at the countryside around me. I wish I could be out there walking, rather than stuck inside this metal box. My hosts are trying to be nice to me, but I'm distracted, stoically accepting this 'special tourist programme'. They finally give up their attempts to make conversation, and we drive on in silence.

Fifty minutes later (I knew it!), we arrive at a small town and head for the packed church. I notice that everyone is in suit and tie; it's obviously a very formal occasion, and I feel ridiculous in my T-shirt and jeans. I get out of the car, and people from the Writers' Union are there waiting for me. They hand me a flower, lead me through the crowd of people attending mass, and we go down some steps behind the altar. I find myself before a tomb. I realize that this is where the saint must be buried; but before I place my flower on the tomb, I want to know who exactly I am paying homage to.

'The Holy Translator,' comes the reply.

The Holy Translator! My eyes fill with tears.

Today is 9 October 2004. The town is called Oshakan, and Armenia, as far as I know, is the only place in the world that has declared the day of the Holy Translator, St Mesrob, a national holiday and where they celebrate it in style. As well as creating the Armenian alphabet (the language already existed, but only in spoken form), St Mesrob devoted his life to translating into his mother tongue the most important texts of the period, which were written in Greek, Persian, and Cyrillic. He and his disciples devoted themselves to the enormous task of translating the Bible and the main literary classics of the time. From that moment on, the country's culture gained its own identity, which it has maintained to this day.

The Holy Translator. I hold the flower in my hands and think of all the people I have never met, and perhaps may never have the opportunity to meet, but who, at this moment, have one of my books in their hands, and are doing their best to remain faithful to what I have tried to share with my readers. I think, above all, of my father-in-law, Christiano Monteiro Oiticica (profession: translator), who is today in the company of the angels and of St Mesrob, watching this scene. I remember seeing him hunched over his old typewriter, often complaining about how badly paid translation was (and, alas, still is). He would immediately go on, though, to explain that the real reason he translated was because he wanted to share a knowledge which, but for translators, would never reach his own people.

I say a silent prayer for him, for all those who have helped me with my books, and for those who have allowed me to read books to which I would never otherwise have had access, thus helping – anonymously – to shape my life and my character. When I leave the church, I see some children writing the alphabet with sweets in the shape of letters and with flowers and more flowers.

When Man grew ambitious, God destroyed the Tower of Babel, and everyone began to speak in different tongues. However, in His infinite grace, he also created people to rebuild those bridges, to enable dialogue and the diffusion of human thought. That person, whose name we so rarely take the trouble to notice when we open a foreign book, is the translator.

Before a Lecture

A Chinese writer and myself were preparing to give a talk at a meeting of American booksellers. The Chinese woman, who was extremely nervous, said to me:

'Talking in public is difficult enough, but imagine having to talk about your book in another language!'

I asked her to stop, otherwise I would start getting nervous too, since I had exactly the same problem. Suddenly, she turned round, smiled and said softly:

'It will be all right, don't worry. We're not alone. Look at the name of the bookshop run by the woman sitting behind me.'

On the woman's badge was written: 'Bookshop of United Angels'. We both managed to do an excellent presentation of our respective books because the angels gave us the sign we were hoping for.

On Elegance

$\mathcal{S}$ ometimes, I find myself sitting or standing with my shoulders hunched. Whenever that happens, I am sure there is something that is not quite right. At that moment, before even trying to find out why I'm feeling uncomfortable, I try to change my posture, to make it more elegant. When I draw myself up again, I realize that this simple movement has helped me to feel more confident about what I'm doing.

Elegance is usually confused with superficiality and fashion. That is a grave mistake. Human beings should be elegant in their actions and their posture, because the word is synonymous with good taste, graciousness, balance, and harmony.

Before taking life's most important steps, we must be both serene and elegant. We must not, of course, become obsessed, worrying all the time about how we move our hands, sit down, smile, look around; but it is good to know that our body is speaking a language, and that the other person – even if only unconsciously – is understanding what we are saying beyond our words.

Serenity comes from the heart. Although often tormented by thoughts of insecurity, the heart knows that, through correct posture, it can regain its equilibrium. The physical elegance I'm talking about comes from the body and is not a superficial thing, but our way of honouring how we place our two feet on the ground. That is why, whenever you feel uncomfortable in that correct posture, you should not think that it is false or artificial. It is true because it is difficult. It makes the path feel honoured by the dignity of the pilgrim.

And please do not confuse it with arrogance or snobbery. Elegance is the right posture to make our every gesture perfect, our steps firm, and to give due respect to our fellow men and women.

Elegance is achieved when all superfluous things have been discarded and the human being discovers simplicity and concentration. The simpler and more sober the posture, the more beautiful it will be.

Snow is beautiful because it has only one colour; the sea is beautiful because it seems to be a flat surface. But both the sea and the snow are deep, and know their own qualities.

Walk joyfully and with a firm step, without fear of stumbling. Your every step is being accompanied by your allies, who will help you if necessary. But do not forget that your adversary is watching too, and that he knows the difference between a firm hand and a tremulous one. Therefore, if you feel tense, breathe deeply and believe that you feel calm, and through one of those inexplicable miracles, you will be filled with tranquillity.

When you make a decision, and set it in motion, try to review mentally each stage that led you to take that step, but do so without tension, because it is impossible to hold all the rules in your head. With your spirit free, as you review each step, you will become aware of which were the most difficult moments, and how you overcame them. This will be reflected in your body, so pay attention!

To make an analogy with archery, many archers complain that, despite many years of practice, they still feel their heart beating anxiously, their hand trembling, their aim faltering. Archery makes our mistakes more obvious.

On days when you feel out of love with life, your aim will be confused, complicated. You will find that you lack sufficient strength to draw the bow, that you cannot make the bow bend as it should. And when, on that morning, you see that your aim is bad, try to discover the cause of such imprecision. This will force you to confront the problem that is troubling you, but which had been hidden up until then.

You discovered the problem because your body was feeling older and less elegant. Change your posture, relax your head, stretch your spine, face the world with an open chest. When you think about your body, you are also thinking about your soul, and one will help the other.

Nhá Chica of Baependi

What is a miracle?

There is a definition for every kind of miracle. It may be something that goes against the laws of nature, an act of divine intervention at a moment of great crisis, something that is considered scientifically impossible, etc.

I have my own definition: a miracle is something that fills the soul with peace. Sometimes it manifests itself in the form of a cure, or a wish granted. It doesn't matter. The end result is that, when the miracle occurs, we feel a profound reverence for the grace God has granted us.

Twenty or more years ago, when I was going through my hippie phase, my sister asked me to be godfather to her first daughter. I was thrilled, and was especially pleased that she did not ask me to cut my hair (at the time, it was almost down to my waist), nor demand an expensive christening present (I didn't have any money to buy one).

The baby was born, a year went by, and no christening. I thought perhaps my sister had changed her mind and so I went to ask her what had happened. She replied: 'You're still the godfather. It's just that I made a promise to Nhá Chica and I want to have her christened in Baependi, because she granted a wish I made.'

I didn't know where Baependi was, and I had never even heard of Nhá Chica. My hippie phase passed, and I became an executive working for a record company. My sister had another child, and still no christening. Finally, in 1978, a decision was taken, and the two families, hers and that of her ex-husband, went to Baependi. There I learned that Nhá Chica, who did not have enough money to keep herself, had spent the last thirty years building a church and helping the poor.

I was going through a very turbulent period in my life and no longer believed in God, or, rather, I no longer believed that the spiritual world was very important. What mattered were the things of this world and what you could achieve here. I had abandoned the mad dreams of my youth – amongst them the dream of becoming a writer – and I had no intention of going back to that dream-world. I was in that church merely to fulfil a social duty. While I was waiting for the christening to begin, I started wandering around outside and ended up going into Nhá Chica's humble little house next to the church. Two rooms, a small altar with a few images of saints, and a vase containing two red roses and one white one.

On an impulse, quite out of keeping with my thinking at the time, I made a promise: *If, one day, I manage to become the writer I once wanted to be, I will come back here when I'm fifty years old and I will bring two red roses and one white one.*

I bought a picture of Nhá Chica, purely as a souvenir of the christening. On the way back to Rio, there was an accident: the bus in front of me suddenly braked and, with split-second timing, I somehow managed to swerve out of the way, as did my brother-in-law; but the car behind us ran straight into the bus, there was an explosion, and several people were killed. We parked at the roadside, not knowing what to do. I reached into my pocket for a cigarette, and there was the picture of Nhá Chica with her silent message of protection.

My journey back to dreams, to the spiritual search and to literature, began right there; and, one day, I found myself once again fighting the Good Fight, the fight you undertake with your heart full of peace, because it is the result of a miracle. I never forgot the three roses. Finally, my fiftieth birthday – which had seemed so far off at the time – arrived.

And it almost passed by. During the World Cup, though, I went to Baependi to fulfil my promise. Someone saw me arriving in Caxambú (where I spent the night), and a journalist came to interview me. When I told him what I was doing, he said:

'Would you like to talk about Nhá Chica. Her body was exhumed this week and the beatification process is with the Vatican now. People should be giving their accounts of their experiences with her.'

'No,' I said. 'It's too personal. I'll only talk about it if I receive a sign.'

And I thought to myself: 'What sign would that be? The only possible sign would be someone speaking on her behalf!'

The next day, I bought the flowers, got into my car, and went to Baependi. I stopped some way from the church, remembering the record company executive who had gone there all those years before, and the many things that had brought me back again. As I was going into the house, a young woman came out of a dress shop and said:

'I noticed that your book *Maktub* is dedicated to Nhá Chica. I bet she was really pleased.'

And she said nothing else. But that was the sign I was waiting for. And this is the public statement I needed to make.

Rebuilding the House

An acquaintance of mine ended up in serious financial difficulties because he could never manage to bring together dream and reality. Worse, he dragged others down with him, harming people he had no wish to harm.

Unable to repay the debts he had accumulated, he even considered suicide. Then one afternoon, as he was walking down a street, he saw a house in ruins. 'That building is me,' he thought, and at that precise moment, he felt an immense desire to rebuild the house.

He found out who the owner was and offered to carry out the necessary work; the owner agreed, although he could not understand what my friend stood to gain. Together they managed to get hold of roof tiles, wood, and cement. My friend put his whole heart into the work, though without knowing why or for whom. But as the renovation work progressed, he felt his personal life improving.

By the end of the year, the house was ready. And all his personal problems had been resolved.

The Prayer That I Forgot

Three weeks ago, I was strolling around São Paulo, when a friend – Edinho – handed me a pamphlet entitled *Sacred Moment*. Printed in four colours, on excellent paper, with no mention of any particular church or religion, this pamphlet bore only a prayer on its reverse side.

Imagine my surprise when I saw the name of the author of this prayer – ME! It had been published in the early 1980s on the inside cover of a book of poetry. I did not think it would stand the test of time, or that it would return to my hands in such a mysterious way; but when I re-read it, I did not feel ashamed of what I had written.

Because it appeared in that pamphlet, and because I believe in signs, I felt it only right to reproduce it here. I hope it encourages every reader to write a prayer of their own, asking for themselves and for others the things that they judge to be most important. That way, we place a positive vibration in our heart that touches everything around us.

Here is the prayer:

Lord, protect our doubts, because Doubt is a way of praying. It is Doubt that makes us grow because it forces us to look fearlessly at the many answers that exist to one question. And in order for this to be possible ...

Lord, protect our decisions, because making Decisions is a way of praying. Give us the courage, after our doubts, to be able to choose between one road and another. May our YES always be a YES, and our NO always be a NO. Once we have chosen our road, may we never look back nor allow our soul to be eaten away by remorse. And in order for this to be possible ...

Lord, protect our actions, because Action is a way of praying. May our daily bread be the result of the very best that we carry within us. May we, through work and Action, share a little of the love we receive. And in order for this to be possible ...

Lord, protect our dreams, because to Dream is a way of praying. Make sure that, regardless of our age or our circumstances, we are capable of keeping alight in our heart the sacred flame of hope and perseverance. And in order for this to be possible ...

Lord, give us enthusiasm, because Enthusiasm is a way of praying. It is what binds us to the Heavens and to Earth, to grown-ups, and to children; it is what tells us that our desires are important and deserve our best efforts. It is Enthusiasm that reaffirms to us that everything is possible, as long as we are totally committed to what we are doing. And in order for this to be possible ...

Lord, protect us, because Life is the only way we have of making manifest Your miracle. May the earth continue to transform seeds into wheat, may we continue to transmute wheat into bread. And this is only possible if we have Love; therefore, do not leave us in solitude. Always give us Your company, and the company of men and women who have doubts, who act and dream and feel enthusiasm, and who live each day as if it were totally dedicated to Your glory.

Amen.

Copacabana, Rio de Janeiro

My wife and I met her on the corner of Rua Constante Ramos in Copacabana. She was about sixty years old, sitting in a wheelchair, lost in the crowd. My wife offered to help her and the woman accepted the offer, asking us to take her to Rua Santa Clara.

There were a few plastic bags hanging from the back of the wheelchair. On the way, she told us that they contained all her belongings. She slept in shop doorways and lived off handouts.

We reached the place where she wanted to go. Other beggars were gathered there. The woman took out two packets of long-life milk from one of the plastic bags and gave it to the other members of the group.

'People are charitable to me, and so I must be charitable to others,' she said.

Living Your Own Legend

I reckon that it takes about three minutes to read each page in this book. Well, according to statistics, in that same space of time, 300 people will die, and another 620 will be born.

I might take half an hour to write each page: I'm sitting at my computer, concentrating on what I'm doing, with books all around me, ideas in my head, cars driving past outside. Everything seems perfectly normal, and yet, during those thirty minutes, 3,000 people have died, and 6,200 have just seen the light of the world for the first time.

Where are those thousands of families who have just begun to mourn the loss of someone, or to smile at the arrival of a son, daughter, nephew, niece, brother, or sister?

I stop and reflect a little. Perhaps many of those people were reaching the end of a long and painful illness, and some people are relieved when the Angel comes for them. Then again, hundreds of those children who have just been born will be abandoned the next moment and will go on to form part of the death statistics before I have even finished writing this page.

How strange. A simple statistic, which I happened to read, and suddenly I'm aware of all those deaths and entrances, those smiles and tears. How many of them are leaving this life while alone in their rooms, with no one realizing what's happening? How many will be born in secret and then abandoned outside a children's home or a convent?

I think to myself that I was once part of the birth statistics and will, one day, be included amongst the numbers of dead. It is good to be aware that I will die. Ever since I walked the road to Santiago, I have understood that, although life goes on and we are all eternal, this existence will one day end.

People do not think very much about death. They spend their lives worrying about absurdities; they put things off, and fail to notice important moments. They don't take risks, because they think it's dangerous. They complain a lot, but are afraid to take action. They want everything to change, but they themselves refuse to change.

If they thought a little more about death, they would never forget to make that much-postponed phone call. They would be a little crazier. They would not be afraid of this incarnation coming to an end, because you cannot fear something that is going to happen anyway.

The Indians say: 'Today is as good a day as any to leave this world.' And a wise man once said: 'Death is always sitting by your side so that, when you need to do something important, it will give you the strength and the courage that you need.'

I hope that you, dear reader, have got this far. It would be foolish to be frightened by death, because all of us, sooner or later, are going to die. And only those who accept this fact are prepared for life.

The Man Who Followed His Dreams

I was born in São José hospital in Rio de Janeiro. It was a fairly difficult birth, and my mother dedicated me to São José, asking him to help me to survive. José – or Joseph – has become a cornerstone of my life. Every year since 1987, the year after my pilgrimage to Santiago de Compostela, I have given a party in his honour, on 19 March. I invite friends and other honest, hard-working people, and before we have supper, we pray for all those who try to preserve the dignity of what they do. We pray, too, for those who are unemployed and with no prospects for the future.

In my little introduction to the prayer, I like to remind people that the word 'dream' appears in the New Testament only five times, and that four out of those five times the word is used in reference to Joseph the carpenter. In all of these cases, he is always being persuaded by an angel to do exactly the opposite of what he was planning to do.

The angel asks him not to abandon his wife, even though she is pregnant. Joseph could say something along the lines of, 'What will the neighbours think?' But he goes back home and believes in the revealed word.

The angel tells him to go into Egypt. His answer could well have been: 'I've got a carpentry business here and regular customers, I can't just abandon it all.' And yet he gathers his things together and heads off into the unknown.

The angel asks him to return from Egypt. Joseph could have thought: 'What, now, when I've just managed to create a settled life again, and when I've got a family to support?'

Joseph goes against what common sense tells him to do and follows his dreams. He knows that he has a destiny to fulfil, which is the destiny of all men on this planet – to protect and support his family. Like millions of anonymous Josephs, he tries to carry out this task, even if it means doing things that are beyond his comprehension.

Later, both his wife and one of his children are transformed into the cornerstones of Christianity. The third pillar of the family, the labourer, is only remembered in nativity scenes at Christmas, or by those who feel a special devotion to him – as I do, and as does Leonardo Boff, for whom I wrote the preface to his book on the carpenter.

I give below part of an article by the writer Carlos Heitor Cony, which I came across on the internet:

> People are sometimes surprised that, given my declared agnosticism and my refusal to accept the idea of a philosophical, moral or religious God, I am, nevertheless, devoted to certain saints in our traditional calendar. God is too distant a concept or entity for my uses or even for my needs. Saints, on

the other hand, with whom I share the same clay foundations, deserve more than my admiration, they deserve my devotion.

St Joseph is one of them. The Gospels do not record a single word spoken by him, only gestures and one explicit reference: *vir justus* – a just man. Since he was a carpenter and not a judge, one must deduce that Joseph was, above all else, good. A good carpenter, a good husband, a good father to the boy who would divide the history of the world.

Beautiful words from Cony. And yet I often read such aberrant statements as: 'Jesus went to India to learn from the teachers in the Himalayas.' I believe that any man can transform the task given him by life into something sacred, and Jesus learned while Joseph, the just man, taught him to make tables, chairs, and beds.

In my imagination, I like to think that the table at which Christ consecrated the bread and the wine would have been made by Joseph, because it must have been the work of some anonymous carpenter, one who earned his living by the sweat of his brow, and who, precisely because of that, allowed miracles to be performed.

The Importance of the Cat in Meditation

When I wrote *Veronika Decides to Die*, a book about madness, I was forced to ask myself how many of the things we do are really necessary, and how many are simply absurd. Why do we wear ties? Why do clocks move clockwise? If we live with a decimal system, why does the day have 24 hours of 60 minutes each?

The fact is that many of the rules we obey nowadays have no real foundation. Nevertheless, if we choose to behave differently, we are considered 'mad' or 'immature'.

As long as this goes on, society will continue to create systems that, with the passing of time, will cease to make any sense, but will continue imposing their rules on us. An interesting Japanese story illustrates my point.

A great Zen master, in charge of the monastery of Mayu Kagi, owned a cat, who was the real love of his life. During meditation classes, he always kept the cat by his side, in order to enjoy its company as much as possible.

One morning, the master, who was already quite old, was found dead. The oldest disciple took his place.

'What shall we do with the cat?' asked the other monks.

In homage to the memory of his former teacher, the new master decided to allow the cat to continue attending the classes on Zen Buddhism.

Some disciples from neighbouring monasteries, who travelled widely in the region, discovered that, in one of the most famous temples in the area, a cat took part in the meditations. The story began to spread.

Many years passed. The cat died, but the students at the monastery were so used to its presence that they acquired another cat. Meanwhile, other temples began introducing cats into their meditation classes; they believed that the cat was the one actually responsible for Mayu Kagi's fame, and for the quality of its teaching, forgetting what an excellent teacher the former master had been.

A generation passed, and technical treatises on the importance of the cat in Zen meditation began to be published. A university professor developed a thesis, accepted by the academic community, that the cat had the ability to increase human concentration and to eliminate negative energy.

And thus, for a century, the cat was considered to be an essential part of the study of Zen Buddhism in that region.

Then a master arrived who was allergic to cat hair, and he decided to remove the cat from his daily practices with the students.

Everyone protested, but the master insisted. Since he was a gifted teacher, the students continued to make progress, despite the cat's absence.

Gradually, monasteries – always in search of new ideas and weary of having to feed so many cats – began to remove cats from the classroom. Over the next twenty years, revolutionary new theses were written, bearing persuasive titles like 'The Importance of Meditating Without a Cat' or 'Balancing the Zen Universe by the Power of One's Mind Alone and Without the Aid of Animals'.

Another century passed, and the cat vanished completely from the Zen meditation ritual in that region. But it took two hundred years for everything to return to normal, and all because, during that time, no one thought to ask why the cat was there.

How many of us, in our own lives, ever dare to ask: why do I behave in such and such a way? In what we do, how far are we, too, using futile 'cats' that we do not have the courage to get rid of because we were told that the 'cats' were important in order to keep everything running smoothly?

Why do we not find a different way of behaving?

I Can't Get In

Near Olite, in Spain, there is a ruined castle. I decide to visit the place and, as I am standing there before it, a man at the door says:

'You can't come in.'

My intuition tells me that he is saying this purely for the pleasure of saying 'No'. I explain that I've come a long way; I try offering him a tip; I try being nice; I point out that this is, after all, a ruined castle. Suddenly, going into that castle has become very important to me.

'You can't come in,' the man says again.

There is only one alternative: to carry on and see if he will physically prevent me from going in. I walk towards the door. He looks at me, but does nothing.

As I am leaving, two other tourists arrive and they, too, walk in. The old man does not try to stop them. I feel as if, thanks to my resistance, the old man has decided to stop inventing ridiculous rules. Sometimes the world asks us to fight for things we do not understand, and whose significance we will never discover.

Statutes for the New Millennium

1 We are all different, and should do what we can to remain so.

2 Each human being was given two possibilities: action and contemplation. Both lead to the same place.

3 Each human being was given two qualities: power and the gift. Power directs us towards our destiny; the gift obliges us to share with others what is best in us.

4 Each human being was given a virtue: the ability to choose. Anyone who fails to use this virtue transforms it into a curse, and others will choose for them.

5 Each human being has his or her own sexual identity and should be able to exercise that identity without guilt as long as they do not force that sexual identity on others.

6 Every human being has a personal legend to be fulfilled, and this is our reason for being in the world. This personal legend manifests itself in our enthusiasm for the task.

7 One can abandon one's personal legend for a time, as long as one does not forget about it entirely and returns to it as soon as possible.

8 Every man has a feminine side, and every woman a masculine side. It is important to use discipline with intuition, and to use intuition with objectivity.

9 Every human being should know two languages: the language of society and the language of signs. One serves to communicate with other people, the other serves to understand God's messages.

10 Every human being has the right to search for happiness, and by 'happiness' is meant something that makes that individual feel content, not necessarily something that makes other people feel content.

11 Every human being should keep alive within them the sacred flame of madness, but should behave as a normal person.

12 Only the following items should be considered to be grave faults: not respecting another's rights; allowing oneself to be paralysed by fear; feeling guilty; believing that one does not deserve the good or ill that happens in one's life; being a coward.

We will love our enemies, but not make alliances with them. They were placed in our path in order to test our sword, and we should, out of respect for them, struggle against them.

We will choose our enemies.

13 All religions lead to the same God, and all deserve the same respect.

Anyone who chooses a religion is also choosing a collective way of worshipping and sharing the mysteries. Nevertheless, that person is the only one responsible for his or her actions along the way and has no right to shift responsibility for any personal decisions on to that religion.

14 It is hereby decreed that the wall separating the sacred and the profane be torn down. From now on, everything is sacred.

15 Everything that is done in the present affects the future in the form of consequence and affects the past in the form of redemption.

16 All statutes to the contrary are revoked.

Destroying and Rebuilding

I am invited to go to Guncan-Gima, the site of a Zen Buddhist temple. When I get there, I'm surprised to see that the extraordinarily beautiful building, which is situated in the middle of a vast forest, is right next to a huge piece of waste ground.

I ask what the waste ground is for and the man in charge explains:

'That is where we will build the next temple. Every twenty years, we destroy the temple you see before you now and rebuild it again on the site next to it. This means that the monks who have trained as carpenters, stonemasons, and architects are always using their practical skills and passing them on to their apprentices. It also shows them that nothing in this life is eternal, and that even temples are in need of constant improvement.'

The Warrior and Faith

Henry James compares experience to a kind of huge spider's web suspended in the chamber of consciousness and capable of trapping not only what is necessary, but every air-borne particle as well.

Often what we call 'experience' is merely the sum of our defeats. Thus we look ahead with the fear of someone who has already made a lot of mistakes in life and we lack the courage to take the next step.

At such moments, it is good to remember the words of Lord Salisbury: 'If you believe the doctors, nothing is wholesome: if you believe the theologians, nothing is innocent: if you believe the soldiers, nothing is safe.'

It is important to accept one's passions, and not to lose one's enthusiasm for conquests. They are part of life, and bring joy to all who participate in them. The warrior of light never loses sight of what endures, nor of bonds forged over time. He knows how to distinguish between the transient and the enduring. There comes a moment, however, when his passions suddenly disappear. Despite all his knowledge, he allows himself to be overwhelmed by despair: from one moment to the next, his faith is not what it was, things do not happen as he dreamed they would, tragedies occur in unfair and unexpected ways, and he begins to believe that his prayers are not being heeded. He continues to pray and to attend religious services, but he cannot deceive himself; his heart does not respond as it once did, and the words seem meaningless.

At such a moment, there is only one possible path to follow: keep practising. Say your prayers out of duty or fear, or for some other reason, but keep praying. Keep on, even if all seems in vain.

The angel in charge of receiving your words, and who is also responsible for the joy of faith, has wandered off somewhere. However, he will soon be back and will only know where to find you if he or she hears a prayer or a request from your lips.

According to legend, after an exhausting morning session of prayer in the monastery of Piedra, the novice asked the abbot if prayers brought God closer to mankind.

'I'm going to reply with another question,' said the abbot. 'Will all the prayers you say make the sun rise tomorrow?'

'Of course not! The sun rises in obedience to a universal law.'

'Well, there's the answer to your question. God is close to us regardless of how much we pray.'

The novice was shocked.

'Are you saying that our prayers are useless?'

'Absolutely not. If you don't wake up early enough, you will never get to see the sunrise. And although God is always close, if you don't pray, you will never manage to feel His presence.'

Watch and pray: that should be the warrior of light's motto. If he only watches, he will start to see ghosts where they don't exist. If he only prays, he will not have time to carry out the work that the world so desperately needs. According to another legend, this time from the *Verba Seniorum*, the abbot pastor used to say that Abbot John had prayed so much that he need no longer worry – all his passions had been vanquished.

The abbot pastor's words reached the ears of one of the wise men in the Monastery of Sceta. He called together the novices after supper.

'You may have heard it said that Abbot John has no more temptations to conquer,' he said. 'However, a lack of struggle weakens the soul. Let us ask the Lord to send Abbot John a great temptation, and if he manages to conquer it, let us ask the Lord to send him another, and another. And when he is once more struggling against temptations, let us pray that he may never say: "Lord, remove this demon from me." Let us pray that he asks: "Lord, give me strength to confront evil."'

In Miami Harbour

'Sometimes, people get so used to what they see in films that they end up forgetting the real story,' says a friend, as we stand together looking out over Miami harbour. 'Do you remember *The Ten Commandments*?'

'Of course I do. At one point, Moses – Charlton Heston – lifts up his rod, the waters part, and the children of Israel cross over.'

'In the Bible it's different,' says my friend. 'There, God says to Moses: "Speak unto the children of Israel, that they go forward." And only afterwards does he tell Moses to lift up his rod, and then the Red Sea parts. It is only courage on the path itself that makes the path appear.'

Acting on Impulse

Father Zeca, from the Church of the Resurrection in Copacabana, tells of how, when he was travelling once on a bus, he suddenly heard a voice telling him to get up and preach the word of Christ right there and then.

Zeca started talking to the voice: 'They'll think I'm ridiculous. This isn't the place for a sermon,' he said. But something inside him insisted that he speak. 'I'm too shy, please don't ask me to do this,' he begged.

The inner impulse insisted.

Then he remembered his promise – to surrender himself to all Christ's purposes. He got up, cringing with embarrassment, and began to talk about the Gospel. Everyone listened in silence. He looked at each passenger in turn, and very few looked away. He said everything that was in his heart, ended his sermon, and sat down again.

He still does not know what task he fulfilled that day, but he is absolutely certain that he did fulfil a task.

Transitory Glory

S *ic transit gloria mundi.* That is how St Paul defines
the human condition in one of his Epistles: 'Thus
passes away the glory of the world.' And yet, knowing
this, we all set off in search of recognition for our work.
Why? One of Brazil's greatest poets, Vinicius de
Moraes, says in the words to a song:

> *E no entanto é preciso cantar,*
> *mais que nunca é preciso cantar.*
> [And meanwhile, we must sing,
> more than ever, we must sing.]

Gertrude Stein said that, 'A rose is a rose is a rose',
but Vinicius de Moraes says only that we must sing.
Brilliant. He gives no explanations, no justifications,
and uses no metaphors. When I stood for the
Brazilian Academy of Letters, I went through the ritual of getting in touch with the other members, and
one academician, Josué Montello, said something
rather similar. He told me: 'Everyone has a duty to
follow the road that passes through his or her village.'

Why? What is there along that road?

What is the force that propels us far from the comfort of all that is familiar and makes us face challenges,

even though we know that the glory of the world will pass away?

I believe that this impulse is the search for the meaning of life.

For many years, I sought a definitive answer to this question in books, in art, in science, in the many dangerous and comfortable roads I have travelled. I found many answers, some of which lasted me for years, and others that failed to withstand even a single day's analysis; and yet none of them was strong enough for me to be able to say: this is the meaning of life.

Now I am convinced that the answer will never be vouchsafed to us in this life, but that, at the end, when we stand once more before the Creator, we will understand each opportunity that was offered to us, which we either accepted or rejected.

In a sermon of 1890, the pastor Henry Drummond speaks of this encounter with the Creator. He says:

The test of man then is not, 'How have I believed?' but 'How have I loved?' The final test of religion is not religiousness, but love: not what I have done, not what I have believed, not what I have achieved, but how I have discharged the common charities of life. Sins of commission in that awful indictment are not even referred to. By what we have not done, *by sins of omission,* we are judged. It could not be otherwise. For the withholding of love is the negation of the Spirit of Christ, the proof that we never knew Him, that for us He lived in vain.

The glory of the world is transitory, and we cannot measure our lives by it, only by the decision we make to follow our personal legend, to believe in our utopias, and to fight for them. Each of us is the protagonist of our own life, and often it is the anonymous heroes who leave the most enduring marks.

A Japanese legend tells how a certain monk, filled with enthusiasm for the beauty of the Chinese book, the *Tao te Ching*, decided to raise enough money to translate and publish it in his own language. This took him ten years.

Meanwhile, his country was devastated by a terrible plague, and the monk decided to use the money he had raised to relieve the suffering of those who were ill. However, as soon as the situation stabilized, he again set about collecting the money he needed to translate and publish the *Tao*. Another ten years passed, and he was just about to publish the book when a tidal wave left hundreds of people homeless.

The monk again spent the money he had collected, this time on rebuilding the homes of those who had lost everything. Another ten years passed; he collected more money and, finally, the Japanese people were able to read the *Tao te Ching*.

Wise men say that, in fact, this monk published three editions of the *Tao*: two invisible and one in print. He believed in his utopia, he fought the good fight, he kept faith with his objective, but he never forgot to look after his fellow human beings. That is how it should be for all of us – sometimes the invisible books, born out of our generosity towards other people, are as important as those that fill our libraries.

Charity Under Threat

S ome time ago, my wife went to the aid of a Swiss tourist in Ipanema, who claimed he had been robbed by some street children. Speaking appalling Portuguese in a thick foreign accent, he said that he had been left without his passport, without any money, and with nowhere to sleep.

My wife bought him lunch, gave him enough cash to pay for a hotel room for the night while he got in touch with his embassy, and then left. Days later, a Rio newspaper reported that this 'Swiss tourist' was, in fact, an inventive con-artist who put on an accent and abused the good faith of those of us who love Rio and want to undo the negative image – justified or not – that has become our postcard.

When she read the article, my wife simply said: 'Well, that's not going to stop me helping anyone.'

Her remark reminded me of the story of a wise man who moved to the city of Akbar. No one took much notice of him, and his teachings were not taken up by the populace. After a time, he became the object of their mockery and their ironic comments.

One day, while he was walking down the main street in Akbar, a group of men and women began insulting him. Instead of pretending that he had not noticed, the wise man turned to them and blessed them.

One of the men said:

'Are you deaf too? We call you the foulest of names and yet you respond with sweet words!'

'We can each of us only offer what we have,' came the wise man's reply.

On Witches and Forgiveness

On 31 October 2004, taking advantage of certain ancient feudal powers that were due to be abolished the following month, the town of Prestonpans in Scotland granted official pardons to eighty-one people – and their cats – who were executed in the sixteenth and seventeenth centuries for practising witchcraft.

According to the official spokeswoman for the Barons Courts of Prestoungrange and Dolphinstoun: 'Most of those persons condemned ... were convicted on the basis of spectral evidence – that is to say, prosecuting witnesses declared that they felt the presence of evil spirits or heard spirit voices.'

There is no point now in going into all the excesses of the Inquisition, with its torture chambers and its bonfires lit by hatred and vengeance; but there is one thing that greatly intrigues me about this story.

The town, and the 14th Baron of Prestoungrange and Dolphinstoun, are granting pardons to people who were brutally executed. Here we are in the twenty-first century, and yet the descendants of the real criminals, those who killed the innocent victims, still feel they have the right to grant pardons.

Meanwhile, a new witch-hunt is starting to gain ground. This time the weapon is not the red-hot iron, but irony and repression. Anyone who develops a gift (which they have usually discovered purely by chance), and dares to speak of their abilities is, more often than not, regarded with distrust, or forbidden by their parents, husband, or wife from saying anything about it. Having been interested since my youth in what are known as 'the occult sciences', I have come into contact with many of these people.

I have, of course, been taken in by charlatans; I have dedicated time and enthusiasm to 'teachers' who eventually dropped their mask and revealed the total void beneath. I have participated irresponsibly in certain sects, and practised rituals for which I have paid a high price. And I did all this in the name of a search that is absolutely natural to humankind: the search for an answer to the mystery of life.

However, I also met many people who really were capable of dealing with forces that went far beyond my comprehension. I have seen the weather being changed, for example; I have seen operations performed without anaesthetic, and on one such occasion (on a day, in fact, when I had woken up feeling full of doubts about our unknown powers) I stuck my finger into an incision made with a rusty penknife. Believe me if you like – or laugh at me if that is the only way you can read what I am writing – but I have seen the transmutation of base metal; I have seen spoons being bent; and lights shining in the air around me because someone said this was going to happen (and it did). These things have almost always occurred with witnesses present, usually sceptical ones. Mostly, those witnesses remained sceptical, always believing that it was all just an elaborate trick. Others said it was 'the Devil's work'.

A few felt that they were witnessing phenomena that went beyond human comprehension.

I have seen this in Brazil, in France, in England, Switzerland, Morocco, and Japan. And what happens with the majority of these people who manage, shall we say, to interfere with the 'immutable' laws of nature? Society considers them to be marginal phenomena; if they can't be explained, then they don't exist. Most of the people themselves can't understand why they are capable of doing these surprising things, and, for fear of being labelled charlatans, they end up suppressing their own gifts.

None of them is happy. They all hope for the day when they can be taken seriously. They all hope for some scientific explanation of their powers (although, in my view, that is not the way forward). Many hide their potential and suffer because of that – because they could help the world, but are not allowed to. Deep down, I think they, too, are waiting to be granted an 'official pardon' for being different.

While separating the wheat from the chaff, and not allowing ourselves to be discouraged by the enormous number of charlatans in the world, I think we should ask ourselves again: what are we capable of? And then, quite calmly, go off in search of our own immense potential.

On Rhythm and the Road

'There was something you didn't mention in your talk about the Road to Santiago,' said a pilgrim as we were leaving the Casa de Galicia, in Madrid, where I had given a lecture only minutes before.

I'm sure there were many things I didn't mention, since my intention had been merely to share something of my own experiences. Nevertheless, I invited her for a cup of coffee, intrigued to know what this important omission was.

And Begoña – for that was her name – said:

'I've noticed that most pilgrims, whether on the Road to Santiago or on any of life's paths, always try to follow the rhythm set by others. At the start of my pilgrimage, I tried to keep up with my group, but I got tired. I was demanding too much of my body. I was tense all the time and ended up straining the tendons in my left foot. I couldn't walk for two days after that, and I realized that I would only reach Santiago if I obeyed my own rhythm. I took longer than the others to get there, and for long stretches I often had to walk alone; but it was only by respecting my own rhythm that I managed to complete the journey. Ever since then, I have applied this to everything I do in life: I follow my own rhythm.'

Travelling Differently

I realized very early on that, for me, travelling was the best way of learning. I still have a pilgrim soul, and I thought that I would pass on some of the lessons I have learned, in the hope that they might prove useful to other pilgrims like me.

1. Avoid museums. This might seem to be absurd advice, but let's just think about it a little. If you are in a foreign city, isn't it far more interesting to go in search of the present than the past? It's just that people feel obliged to go to museums because they learned as children that travelling was about seeking out that kind of culture. Obviously, museums are important, but they require time and objectivity – you need to know what you want to see there, otherwise you will leave with a sense of having seen a few really fundamental things, but can't remember what they were.

2. Hang out in bars. Bars are the places where life in the city reveals itself, not in museums. By bars I don't mean discotheques, but the places where ordinary people go, have a drink, ponder the weather, and are always ready for a chat. Buy a newspaper and enjoy the ebb and flow of people. If someone strikes up a conversation, however silly, join in: you cannot judge the beauty of a particular path just by looking at the gate.

3. Be open. The best tour guide is someone who lives in the place, knows everything about it, is proud of his or her city, but does not work for any agency. Go out into the street, choose the person you want to talk to, and ask them something (Where is the cathedral? Where is the post office?). If nothing comes of it, try someone else – I guarantee that by the end of the day you will have found yourself an excellent companion.

4. Try to travel alone or – if you are married – with your spouse. It will be harder work, no one will be there taking care of you, but only in this way can you truly leave your own country behind. Travelling with a group is a way of being in a foreign country while speaking your mother tongue, doing whatever the leader of the flock tells you to do, and taking more interest in group gossip than in the place you are visiting.

5. Don't compare. Don't compare anything – prices, standards of hygiene, quality of life, means of transport, nothing! You are not travelling in order to prove that you have a better life than other people. Your aim is to find out how other people live, what they can teach you, how they deal with reality and with the extraordinary.

6. Understand that everyone understands you. Even if you don't speak the language, don't be afraid. I've been in lots of places where I could not communicate with words at all, and I always found support, guidance, useful advice, and even girlfriends. Some people think that if they travel alone, they will set off down the street and be lost for ever. Just make sure you have the hotel card in your pocket and – if the worst comes to the worst – flag down a taxi and show the card to the driver.

7. Don't buy too much. Spend your money on things you won't need to carry: tickets to a good play, restaurants, trips. Nowadays, with the global economy and the internet, you can buy anything you want without having to pay excess baggage.

8. Don't try to see the world in a month. It is far better to stay in a city for four or five days than to visit five cities in a week. A city is like a capricious woman: she takes time to be seduced and to reveal herself completely.

9. A journey is an adventure. Henry Miller used to say that it is far more important to discover a church that no one else has ever heard of than to go to Rome and feel obliged to visit the Sistine Chapel with two hundred thousand other tourists bellowing in your ear. By all means go to the Sistine Chapel, but wander the streets too, explore alleyways, experience the freedom of looking for something – quite what you don't know, but which, if you find it, will, you can be sure, change your life.

A Fairy Tale

Maria Emilia Voss, a pilgrim to Santiago, tells the following story.

In ancient China, around the year 250 BC, a certain prince of the region of Thing-Zda was about to be crowned emperor; however, according to the law, he first had to get married.

Since this meant choosing the future empress, the prince needed to find a young woman whom he could trust absolutely. On the advice of a wise man, he decided to summon all the young women of the region in order to find the most worthy candidate.

An old lady, who had served in the palace for many years, heard about the preparations for this gathering and felt very sad, for her daughter nurtured a secret love for the prince.

When the old lady got home, she told her daughter and was horrified to learn that she intended going to the palace.

The old lady was desperate.

'But, daughter, what on earth will you do there? All the richest and most beautiful girls from the court will be present. It's a ridiculous idea! I know you must be suffering, but don't turn that suffering into madness.'

And the daughter replied:

'My dear mother, I am not suffering and I certainly haven't gone mad. I know that I won't be chosen, but it's my one chance to spend at least a few moments close to the prince, and that makes me happy, even though I know that a quite different fate awaits me.'

That night, when the young woman reached the palace, all the most beautiful girls were indeed there, wearing the most beautiful clothes and the most beautiful jewellery, and prepared to do anything to seize the opportunity on offer.

Surrounded by the members of his court, the prince announced a challenge.

'I will give each of you a seed. In six months' time, the young woman who brings me the loveliest flower will be the future empress of China.'

The girl took her seed and planted it in a pot, and since she was not very skilled in the art of gardening, she prepared the soil with great patience and tenderness, for she believed that if the flowers grew as large as her love, then she need not worry about the results.

Three months passed and no shoots had appeared. The young woman tried everything; she consulted farmers and peasants, who showed her the most varied methods of cultivation, but all to no avail. Each day she felt that her dream had moved farther off, although her love was as alive as ever.

At last, the six months were up, and still nothing had grown in her pot. Even though she had nothing to show, she knew how much effort and dedication she had put in during that time, and so she told her mother that she would go back to the palace on the agreed date and at the agreed hour. Inside, she knew that this would be her last meeting with her true love, and she would not have missed it for the world.

The day of the audience arrived. The girl appeared with her plantless pot, and saw that all the other candidates had achieved wonderful results: each girl bore a flower lovelier than the last, in the most varied forms and colours.

Finally, the longed-for moment came. The prince entered and he studied each of the candidates with great care and attention. Having inspected them all, he announced the result and chose the servant's daughter as his new wife.

All the other girls present began to protest, saying that he had chosen the only one of them who had failed to grow anything at all.

Then the prince calmly explained the reasoning behind the challenge.

'This young woman was the only one who cultivated the flower that made her worthy of becoming the empress: the flower of honesty. All the seeds I handed out were sterile, and nothing could ever have grown from them.'

Brazil's Greatest Writer

I had published, at my own expense, a book entitled *The Archives of Hell* (of which I am very proud, but which is not currently available in bookshops simply because I have not yet found the courage to revise it). We all know how difficult it is to get published, but it is an even more complicated business getting your book into the shops. Every week, my wife would visit the bookshops in one part of the city, whilst I would go to another part to do the same thing.

So one day, she was crossing Avenida Copacabana with some copies of my book under her arm and there, on the other side of the street, were Jorge Amado and his wife Zélia Gattai! Almost without thinking, she went over and told them that her husband was a writer. Jorge and Zélia (who must hear this sort of thing every day) were kindness itself; they invited her to have a coffee with them, asked for a copy of the book, and concluded by sending me their best wishes for my literary career.

'You're mad!' I said, when she came home. 'Don't you know he's the most important writer in Brazil?'

'Exactly,' she said. 'Anyone who has got where he has must have a pure heart.'

A pure heart: Christina could not have spoken a truer word. And Jorge, the most famous Brazilian writer outside of Brazil, was (and is) the great indicator of which way Brazilian literature was going.

One day, however, *The Alchemist*, written by another Brazilian, made it into the bestseller list in France, and in a few weeks it reached number one.

Days later, I received a cutting of the list, along with an affectionate letter from Jorge congratulating me. There is no room in Jorge Amado's pure heart for feelings like jealousy.

Some journalists – from inside and outside Brazil – began trying to provoke him by asking him leading questions. Never, at any time, did Jorge allow himself to take the easy path of destructive criticism; indeed, he became my defender at a very difficult time in my life, when most reviews of my work were extremely harsh.

I finally won my first foreign literary award, in France to be precise. It just so happened that, on the date fixed for the award ceremony, I had a previous commitment in Los Angeles. Anne Carrière, my French publisher, was in despair. She talked to the American publishers, who refused to cancel any of the planned lecture tour.

The date of the award ceremony was approaching, and the prizewinner could not go: what should she do? Without consulting me, Anne phoned Jorge Amado and explained the situation. Jorge immediately offered to go there as my representative.

Not only that, but he telephoned the Brazilian ambassador and invited him along too, and made a wonderful speech that touched the hearts of everyone present.

The oddest thing of all is that I only met Jorge Amado in person nearly a year after the prize-giving.

Ah, but I had already learned to admire his heart as much as I admired his books: a famous author who never despises beginners, a Brazilian who is pleased to see other Brazilians succeed, a human being always ready to help when asked.

The Meeting That Did Not Take Place

I believe that, at least once a week, we all come across a stranger with whom we would like to talk, but we always lack the courage to do so. A few days ago, I received a letter on this subject sent by a reader I will call Antonio. I give below a shortened version of what happened to him.

I was walking along the Gran Vía when I saw a woman – petite, light-skinned, and well-dressed – begging for money from passers-by. As I approached, she asked me for a few coins with which to buy a sandwich. In Brazil, I was used to beggars wearing very old, dirty clothes, and so I decided not to give her anything and walked on. The look she gave me, however, left me with a strange feeling.

I went to my hotel and suddenly felt an incomprehensible urge to go back and give her some money – I was on holiday, I had just had lunch, I had money in my pocket, and it must be terribly humiliating to have to beg in the street and to be stared at by everyone.

I went back to the place where I had seen her. She was no longer there; I searched the nearby streets, but could find no trace of her. The following day, I repeated this pilgrimage, again in vain.

From that day on, I slept only fitfully. I returned to Brazil and told a friend about my experience. She said that I had failed to make some very important connection and advised me to ask for God's help. I prayed, and seemed to hear a voice saying that I needed to find the beggar-woman again. I kept waking up in the night, sobbing. I realized that I could not go on like this, and so I scraped together enough money to buy a ticket back to Madrid in order to look for the beggar-woman.

I began a seemingly endless search, to which I devoted myself entirely; but time was passing, and my money was running out. I had to go to the travel agent's to change my flight date home, having resolved not to go back to Brazil until I had given the woman the money I had failed to give her on that first meeting.

As I was coming out of the travel agent's, I stumbled on a step and collided with someone – it was the woman I was looking for.

I automatically put my hand in my pocket, took out all the money I had in there, and held it out to her. I felt a profound sense of peace, and thanked God for that second wordless meeting, for that second chance.

I have been back to Spain several times since, and I know that I will never meet her again; but I did what my heart demanded.

The Smiling Couple
(London, 1977)

I was married to a young woman called Cecília and – at a period in my life when I had decided to give up everything for which I no longer felt any enthusiasm – we had gone to live in London. We stayed in a small, second-floor flat in Palace Street and were having great difficulty making new friends. However, every night, a young couple would leave the pub next door and walk past our window waving and calling to us to come down.

I was extremely worried about bothering the neighbours, and so I never went down, pretending, instead, that it had nothing to do with me. But the couple kept calling up to us, even when there was no one at the window.

One night, I did go down to complain about the noise. Their laughter immediately turned to sadness; they apologized, and went away. That night, I realized that, although we very much wanted to make new friends, I was far more concerned about 'what the neighbours would say'.

I decided that the next time, I would invite the couple up to have a drink with us. I waited all week at the window, at the time they usually passed, but they never came back. I started going to the pub in the hope of seeing them, but the owner of the pub claimed not to know them.

I placed a notice in the window saying: 'Call again.' All this achieved was that, one night, a group of drunks began hurling every swearword under the sun at our window, and our neighbour – the one I had been so worried about – ended up complaining to the landlord.

I never saw the couple again.

The Second Chance

'I've always been fascinated by the story of the Sybilline books,' I said to Mônica, my friend and literary agent, while we were driving to Portugal, 'which is about the importance of seizing every opportunity while it's there, and how if you don't, it's lost for ever.'

The Sibyls, who were prophetesses capable of foreseeing the future, lived in Ancient Rome. One day, one of them came to the Emperor Tiberius' palace bearing nine books. She claimed that they contained the future of the Empire and asked for ten gold talents in payment. Tiberius thought this far too expensive and refused to buy them.

The Sibyl left, burned three of the books, and returned with the remaining six. 'They still cost ten gold talents,' she said. Tiberius laughed and sent her away. How did she have the nerve to sell six books for the price of nine?

The Sibyl burned three more of the books and went back to Tiberius with the three remaining volumes. 'They still cost ten gold talents,' she said. Intrigued, Tiberius ended up buying the three volumes, but he could only read in them a little of what the future held.

When I had finished telling the story, I realized that we were passing through Ciudad Rodrigo, close to the border between Spain and Portugal. There, four years earlier, I had been offered a book, but had declined to buy it.

'Let's stop here. I think that remembering the Sybilline books was a sign for me to put right a mistake I made in the past.'

During the first tour I made of Europe publicizing my books, I had had lunch in Ciudad Rodrigo. Afterwards, I visited the cathedral and met a priest. 'Doesn't the inside of the church look lovely in the afternoon sun,' he said. I liked this remark; we talked a little, and he showed me round the church's altars and cloisters and inner gardens. In the end, he offered me a book he had written about the church, but I chose not to buy it. When I left, I felt guilty; after all, I'm a writer, and there I was in Europe trying to sell my work, so why not buy the priest's book out of solidarity? Then I forgot all about the episode, until that moment.

I stopped the car, and Mônica and I walked across the square in front of the church, where a woman was looking up at the sky.

'Good afternoon,' I said, 'I'm looking for a priest who wrote a book about this church.'

'Oh, you mean Father Stanislau. He died a year ago,' she replied.

I felt terribly sad. Why had I not given Father Stanislau the same joy I feel whenever I see someone reading one of my own books?

'He was one of the kindest men I've ever known,' the woman went on. 'He came from a very humble family, but became an expert in archaeology. He helped my son get a grant to go to university.'

I told her why I was there.

'Don't go blaming yourself over a trifle like that, my dear,' she said. 'Go and visit the church again.'

I thought this was a sign too and so I did as she said. There was only one priest in the confessional, waiting for the faithful who did not come. I went over to him and he indicated that I should kneel down, but I said:

'No, I don't want to confess. I just came to buy a book about this church by a man called Stanislau.'

The priest's eyes lit up. He left the confessional and returned minutes later with a copy of the book.

'How wonderful that you should come here just for this,' he said. 'I'm Father Stanislau's brother, and it makes me really proud. He must be in heaven now, glad to see that his work is considered so important.'

Of all the priests I could have met, I had come across Stanislau's brother. I paid for the book, thanked him, and he embraced me. As I turned to leave, I heard him say:

'Doesn't the inside of the church look lovely in the afternoon sun!'

These were the same words that Father Stanislau had said four years before. Life always gives us a second chance.

The Australian and the Newspaper Ad

I'm in Sydney harbour, looking at the beautiful bridge that joins the two halves of the city, when an Australian comes up to me and asks me to read an advertisement in the newspaper.

'The print is too small,' he says. 'I can't make out what it says.'

I try, but I haven't got my reading glasses with me. I apologize to the man.

'Oh, that's all right,' he says. 'Do you know something? I think that God suffers from poor eyesight too, not because He's old, but because that's how He wants it to be. That way, when someone does something wrong, He can always say He couldn't quite see, and so ends up forgiving the person because He doesn't want to commit an injustice.'

'And what if someone does something good?' I ask.

'Ah, well,' laughs the Australian, moving off, 'God, of course, never leaves His glasses at home!'

The Tears of the Desert

A friend of mine returns from Morocco with a beautiful story about a missionary who, as soon as he arrived in Marrakesh, decided that he would go for a walk every morning in the desert that lay just outside the city. The first time he did this, he noticed a man lying down, with his ear pressed to the ground and stroking the sand with one hand.

'He's obviously mad,' the missionary said to himself.

But the scene was repeated every day, and after a month, intrigued by this strange behaviour, he decided to speak to the stranger. With great difficulty, since he was not yet fluent in Arabic, he knelt down by his side.

'What are you doing?'

'I'm keeping the desert company and offering it consolation for its loneliness and its tears.'

'I didn't know the desert was capable of tears.'

'It weeps every day because it dreams of being useful to people, and of being transformed into a vast garden where they could grow cereal crops and flowers and graze sheep.'

'Well, tell the desert that it is performing an important duty,' said the missionary. 'Whenever I walk in the desert, I understand man's true size, because its vast open space reminds me of how small we are compared with God. When I look at its sands, I imagine all the millions of people in the world who were born equal, even if the world has not always been fair to all of them. Its mountains help me to meditate, and when I see the sun coming up over the horizon, my soul fills with joy and I feel closer to the Creator.'

The missionary left the man and returned to his daily tasks. Imagine his surprise when, next morning, he found the man in the same place and in the same position.

'Did you tell the desert everything that I said?'

The man nodded.

'And it's still weeping?'

'I can hear every sob. Now it's weeping because it has spent thousands of years thinking that it was completely useless and wasted all that time blaspheming against God and its own fate.'

'Well, tell the desert that even though we human beings have a much shorter lifespan, we also spend much of our time thinking we're useless. We rarely discover our true destiny, and feel that God has been unjust to us. When the moment finally comes, and something happens that reveals to us the reason we were born, we think it's too late to change our life and continue to suffer, and, like the desert, blame ourselves for the time we have wasted.'

'I don't know if the desert will hear that,' said the man. 'He's accustomed to pain, and can't see things any other way.'

'Let's do what I always do when I sense that people have lost all hope. Let us pray.'

The two men knelt down and prayed. One turned towards Mecca because he was a Muslim, and the other put his hands together in prayer because he was a Catholic. They each prayed to their own God, who has always been the same God, even though people insist on calling him by different names.

The following day, when the missionary went for his usual morning walk, the man was no longer there. In the place where he used to embrace the earth, the sand seemed wet, for a small spring had started bubbling up there. In the months that followed, the spring grew, and the inhabitants of the city built a well there.

The Bedouin call the place 'The Well of the Desert's Tears'. They say that anyone who drinks from its waters will find a way of transforming the reason for his suffering into the reason for his joy, and will end up finding his true destiny.

Rome: Isabella Returns from Nepal

I meet Isabella in a restaurant where we usually go because it's always empty, even though the food is excellent. She tells me that, during her trip to Nepal, she spent some weeks in a monastery. One afternoon, she was walking near the monastery with one of the monks, when he opened the bag he was carrying and stood for a long time studying its contents. Then he said to Isabella:

'Did you know that bananas can teach you the meaning of life?'

He took out a rotten banana from the bag and threw it away.

'That is the life that has been and gone, and which was not used to the full and for which it is now too late.'

Then he drew out another banana, which was still green. He showed it to her and put it back in the bag.

'This is the life that has yet to happen, and for which we need to wait until the moment is right.'

Finally, he took out a ripe banana, peeled it, and shared it with Isabella.

'This is the present moment. Learn how to gobble it up without fear or guilt.'

The Art of the Sword

Many centuries ago, in the days of the Samurai, a book was written in Japan about the spiritual art of the sword: *Impassive Understanding*, also known as *The Treatise of Tahlan*, which was the name of its author (who was both a fencing master and a Zen monk). I have adapted a few sections below:

Keeping calm. Anyone who understands the meaning of life knows that things have neither a beginning nor an end, and that there is, therefore, no point in worrying. Fight for what you believe in without trying to prove anything to anyone; maintain the same silent calm of someone who has had the courage to choose his own destiny.

This applies to both love and war.

Allowing your heart to be present. Anyone who trusts in his powers of seduction, in his ability to say the right thing at the right time, in the correct use of the body, becomes deaf to the 'voice of the heart'. This can only be heard when we are in complete harmony with the world around us, and never when we judge ourselves to be the centre of the universe.

This applies to both love and war.

Learning to be the other person. We are so focused on what we judge to be the best attitude that we forget something very important: in order to attain our objectives, we need other people. It is necessary, therefore, not only to observe the world, but to imagine ourselves into the skins of other people, and to learn how to follow their thoughts.

This applies to both love and war.

Finding the right master. Our path will always cross that of other people who, out of love or pride, want to teach us something. How can we distinguish the friend from the manipulator? The answer is simple: the true teacher is not the one who teaches us the ideal path, but the one who shows us the many ways of reaching the road we need to travel if we are to find our destiny. Once we have found that road, the teacher cannot help us anymore, because its challenges are unique.

This applies to neither love nor war, but unless we understand it, we will never get anywhere.

Escaping from threats. We often think that the ideal attitude is that of giving up one's life for a dream. Nothing could be further from the truth. In order to achieve a dream, we need to preserve our life, and we must, therefore, know how to avoid those things that threaten us. The more we plan our steps, the more chance there is that we will go wrong, because we are failing to take into consideration four things: other people, life's teachings, passion, and calm. The more we feel we are in control of things, the farther off we are from controlling anything. A threat does not issue any warning, and a swift reaction cannot be planned like a Sunday afternoon walk.

Therefore, if you want to be in harmony with your love or with your fight, learn to react rapidly. Through educated observation, do not allow your supposed experience of life to transform you into a machine. Use that experience to listen always to 'the voice of the heart'. Even if you do not agree with what that voice is saying, respect it and follow its advice: it knows when to act and when to avoid action.

This applies to both love and war.

In the Blue Mountains

The day after my arrival in Australia, my publisher takes me to a natural park close to Sydney. There, in the midst of the forest that covers an area known as the Blue Mountains, are three rock formations in the form of obelisks.

'They're the Three Sisters,' my publisher says, and then tells me the following legend.

A shaman was out walking with his three sisters when the most famous warrior of the time approached them and said:

'I want to marry one of these lovely girls.'

'If one of them marries, the other two will think they're ugly. I'm looking for a tribe where warriors are allowed to have three wives,' replied the shaman, moving off.

For years, the shaman travelled the Australian continent, but never found that tribe.

'At least one of us could have been happy,' said one of the sisters, when they were old and tired of all that walking.

'I was wrong,' said the shaman, 'but now it's too late.'

And he transformed the three sisters into blocks of stone, so that anyone who passed by there would understand that the happiness of one does not mean the unhappiness of the others.

The Taste of Success

Arash Hejazi, my Iranian publisher, tells a story about a man who, in his search for spiritual enlightenment, decided to climb a high mountain dressed only in his normal clothes and to spend the rest of his life there meditating.

He realized at once that one change of clothing wouldn't be enough because his clothes soon became dirty. He came down the mountain, went to the nearest village and begged them to give him some more clothes. Since they all knew he was a man in search of enlightenment, they gave him a new pair of trousers and a new shirt.

The man thanked them and went back up to the hermitage he was building on top of the mountain. He spent his nights building the walls and his days in meditation. He ate the fruit from the trees, and drank the water from a nearby spring.

A month later, he discovered that a mouse was nibbling away at his spare set of clothes, which he had left out to dry. Since he wanted to concentrate exclusively on his spiritual duties, he went down to the village again and asked them to get him a cat. The villagers, who respected his search for spiritual enlightenment, found him a cat.

Seven days later, the cat was close to starvation because it could not live on fruit alone and there were no more mice around. The man went back to the village in search of milk. The villagers knew that the milk was not for him and that he was surviving without eating anything apart from what Nature provided, and so, once again, they helped him.

The cat soon finished the milk, and the man asked the villagers to lend him a cow. Since the cow gave more milk than the cat could drink, the man started drinking it too, so as not to waste it. Soon, by dint of breathing good mountain air, eating fruit, meditating, drinking milk, and doing exercise, he was transformed into a very handsome specimen indeed. A young woman, who had gone up the mountain in search of a sheep, fell in love with him and persuaded him that he needed a wife to take care of the household duties, leaving him free to meditate in peace.

Three years later, the man was married with two children, three cows, and an orchard and was running a meditation centre, with a long waiting list of people wanting to visit the 'Temple of Eternal Youth'.

When someone asked him how it had all started, he said:

'I arrived here with only two items of clothing, and when I had been here for two weeks, a mouse started nibbling one of them and ...'

But no one was interested in the end of the story; they were sure that he was simply an astute business-man trying to invent a legend that would justify him putting up the price of a stay at the temple still more.

The Tea Ceremony

In Japan, I took part in a tea ceremony. You go into a small room, tea is served, and that's it really, except that everything is done with so much ritual and ceremony that a banal daily event is transformed into a moment of communion with the universe.

The tea master, Okakura Kakuzo, explains what happens:

'The ceremony is a way of worshipping the beautiful and the simple. All one's efforts are concentrated on trying to achieve perfection through the imperfect gestures of daily life. Its beauty consists in the respect with which it is performed. If a mere cup of tea can bring us closer to God, we should watch out for all the other dozens of opportunities that each ordinary day offers us.'

The Cloud and the Sand Dune

'As everyone knows, the life of a cloud is very busy and very short,' writes Bruno Ferrero. And here's a related story.

A young cloud was born in the midst of a great storm over the Mediterranean Sea, but he did not even have time to grow up there, for a strong wind pushed all the clouds over towards Africa.

As soon as the clouds reached the continent, the climate changed. A bright sun was shining in the sky and, stretched out beneath them, lay the golden sands of the Sahara. Since it almost never rains in the desert, the wind continued pushing the clouds towards the forests in the south.

Meanwhile, as happens with young humans too, the young cloud decided to leave his parents and his older friends in order to discover the world.

'What are you doing?' cried the wind. 'The desert's the same all over. Rejoin the other clouds, and we'll go to Central Africa where there are amazing mountains and trees!'

But the young cloud, a natural rebel, refused to obey, and, gradually, he dropped down until he found a gentle, generous breeze that allowed him to hover over the golden sands. After much toing and froing, he noticed that one of the dunes was smiling at him.

He saw that the dune was also young, newly formed by the wind that had just passed over. He fell in love with her golden hair right there and then.

'Good morning,' he said. 'What's life like down there?'

'I have the company of the other dunes, of the sun and the wind, and of the caravans that occasionally pass through here. Sometimes it's really hot, but it's still bearable. What's life like up there?'

'We have the sun and wind too, but the good thing is that I can travel across the sky and see more things.'

'For me,' said the dune, 'life is short. When the wind returns from the forests, I will disappear.'

'And does that make you sad?'

'It makes me feel that I have no purpose in life.'

'I feel the same. As soon as another wind comes along, I'll go south and be transformed into rain; but that is my destiny.'

The dune hesitated for a moment, then said:

'Did you know that here in the desert, we call the rain paradise?'

'I had no idea I could ever be that important,' said the cloud proudly.

'I've heard other older dunes tell stories about the rain. They say that, after the rain, we are all covered with grass and flowers. But I'll never experience that, because in the desert it rains so rarely.'

It was the cloud's turn to hesitate now. Then he smiled broadly and said:

'If you like, I could rain on you now. I know I've only just got here, but I love you, and I'd like to stay here for ever.'

'When I first saw you up in the sky, I fell in love with you too,' said the dune. 'But if you transform your lovely white hair into rain, you will die.'

'Love never dies,' said the dune. 'It is transformed, and, besides, I want to show you what paradise is like.'

And he began to caress the dune with little drops of rain, so that they could stay together for longer, until a rainbow appeared.

The following day, the little dune was covered in flowers. Other clouds that passed over, heading for Africa, thought that it must be part of the forest they were looking for and scattered more rain. Twenty years later, the dune had been transformed into an oasis that refreshed travellers with the shade of its trees.

And all because, one day, a cloud fell in love, and was not afraid to give his life for that love.

Norma and the Good Things

In Madrid lives Norma, a very special Brazilian lady. The Spanish call her 'the rocking grandma'. She is over sixty and works in various places, organizing promotions, parties, and concerts.

Once, at about four in the morning, when I was so tired I could barely stand, I asked Norma where she got all her energy from.

'I have a magic calendar. If you like, I can show it to you.'

The following day, I went to her house. She picked up an old, much scribbled-upon calendar.

'Right, today is the day they discovered a vaccine against polio,' she said. 'We must celebrate that, because life is beautiful.'

On each day of the year, Norma had written down something good that had happened on that date. For her, life was always a reason to be happy.

Jordan, the Dead Sea, 21 June 2003

On the table next to mine sat the King and Queen of Jordan; Secretary of State Colin Powell; the Representative of the Arab League; the Israeli Foreign Minister; the President of the German Republic; Hamid Karzai, President of Afghanistan, as well as other notable names involved in the processes of war and peace that we are currently witnessing. Although the temperature was touching 40°C, a gentle breeze was blowing in the desert, a pianist was playing a sonata, the sky was clear, and the place was lit by torches scattered about the garden. On the other side of the Dead Sea, we could see Israel and the glow of Jerusalem's lights on the horizon. In short, all seemed peace and harmony, and suddenly I realized that, far from being an aberration from reality, this moment was what every one of us dreamed of. My pessimism has grown in recent months, but if people can still manage to talk to each other, then all is not lost.

Later, Queen Rania would remark that the place had been chosen for its symbolic significance. The Dead Sea is the lowest body of water on Earth (401 metres below sea level). To go any deeper, you would have to dive; but in the case of the Dead Sea, the water is so salty that it forces the body back up to the surface. It is the same with the long, painful peace process in the Middle East. We cannot get any lower than we are now. If I had turned on the TV that day, I would have learned of the death of a Jewish settler and of a young Palestinian. But there I was, at that supper, with the strange feeling that the calm of that night would spread throughout the region, that people would talk to each other again as they were talking then, that Utopia was possible, that mankind would not sink any lower.

If you ever have the chance to go to the Middle East, be sure to visit Jordan (a marvellous, friendly country), go to the Dead Sea, and look at Israel on the other side. You will understand then that peace is both necessary and possible. Below, I give part of the speech I wrote and read during the event, accompanied by improvisations from the brilliant Jewish violinist Ivry Gitlis.

Peace is not the opposite of war.

We can have peace in our heart even in the midst of the fiercest battles, because we are fighting for our dreams. When our friends have lost hope, the peace of the Good Fight helps us to carry on.

A mother who can feed her child has peace in her eyes, even when her hands are trembling because diplomacy has failed, bombs are falling, and soldiers dying.

An archer drawing his bow has peace in his mind, even though all his muscles are tense with the physical effort.

Therefore, for warriors of light, peace is not the opposite of war, because they are capable of:

a   distinguishing between the transient and the endur-
    ing. They can fight for their dreams and for their
    survival, but respect bonds forged over time,
    through culture and religion.
b   knowing that their adversaries are not necessarily
    their enemies.
c   being aware that their actions will affect five future
    generations, and that their children and grandchil-
    dren will benefit from (or suffer) the consequences.
d   remembering what the *I Ching* says: 'Perseverance is
    favourable.' But they know too that perseverance is
    not the same thing as stubbornness. Battles that go
    on longer than necessary end up destroying the
    enthusiasm necessary for later reconstruction.

For the warrior of light, there are no abstractions. Every
opportunity to transform himself is an opportunity to
transform the world.

For the warrior of light, pessimism does not exist.
He rows against the tide if necessary; for when he is old
and tired, he will be able to say to his grandchildren
that he came into this world to understand his neighbour better, not to condemn his brother.

In San Diego Harbour, California

I was talking to a woman from the Tradition of the Moon – a kind of initiation path for women that works in harmony with the forces of nature.

'Would you like to touch a seagull?' she asked, looking at the birds perched along the sea wall.

Of course I would. I tried several times, but whenever I got close, they would fly away.

'Try to feel love for the bird, then allow that love to pour out of your breast like a ray of light and touch the bird's breast. Then very quietly go over to it.'

I did as she suggested. The first two times I failed, but the third time, as if I had entered a kind of trance, I did touch the seagull. I went into that trance state again with the same positive result.

'Love creates bridges where it would seem they were impossible,' said my white witch friend.

I recount this experience here, for anyone who would like to try it.

The Art of Withdrawal

A warrior of light who trusts too much in his intelligence will end up underestimating the power of his opponent.

It is important not to forget that, sometimes, strength is more effective than strategy. When we are confronted by a certain kind of violence, no amount of brilliance, argument, intelligence, or charm can avert tragedy.

That is why the warrior never underestimates brute force. When it proves too violent, he withdraws from the battlefield until his enemy has exhausted himself.

However, be very clear about one thing: a warrior of light is never cowardly. Flight might be an excellent form of defence, but it cannot be used when one is very afraid.

When in doubt, the warrior prefers to face defeat and then lick his wounds, because he knows that, if he flees, he is giving to the aggressor greater power than he deserves.

The warrior of light can heal the physical suffering, but will be eternally pursued by his spiritual weakness. In difficult and painful times, the warrior faces overwhelming odds with heroism, resignation, and courage.

In order to reach the necessary state of mind (since he is entering a battle in which he is at a disadvantage and could suffer greatly), the warrior of light needs to know exactly what might harm him. Okakura Kakuzo says in his book on the Japanese tea ceremony: 'We see the evil in others because we know the evil in ourselves. We never forgive those who wound us because we believe that we would never be forgiven. We say the painful truth to others because we want to hide it from ourselves. We show our strength, so that no one can see our frailty. That is why, whenever you judge your brother, be aware that it is you who is in the dock.'

Sometimes, this awareness can avoid a fight that will only bring disadvantages. Sometimes, however, there is no way out, only an unequal battle.

'We know we are going to lose, but our enemy and his violence leave us no alternative, apart from cowardice, and that is of no interest to us. At such a moment, it is necessary to accept destiny, trying to keep in mind a text from the wonderful *Bhagavad Gita* (Chapter II, 16-26):

'Man is not born, nor does he die. Having come into existence, he will never cease to be, because he is eternal and permanent.

'Just as a man discards old clothes and puts on new clothes, so the soul discards the old body and puts on a new one.

'But the soul is indestructible; swords cannot pierce it, fire cannot burn it, water cannot wet it, the wind cannot dry it. It is beyond the power of all these things.

'Since man is always indestructible, he is always victorious (even in his defeats), and that is why he should never be sad'.

In the Midst of War

The film-maker Rui Guerra told me that, one night, he was talking with friends in a house in the interior of Mozambique. The country was at war, and so everything – from petrol to electric light – was in short supply.

To pass the time, they started talking about what they would like to eat. Each of them described his or her favourite food; and when it came to Rui's turn, he said: 'I'd like to eat an apple', knowing that, because of rationing, it was impossible to find any fruit at all.

At that precise moment, they heard a noise, and a beautiful, shiny apple rolled into the room and stopped in front of him!

Later, Rui discovered that one of the girls who lived there had gone out to buy some fruit on the black market. As she came up the stairs, she tripped and fell, the bag of apples she had bought split open, and one of the apples had rolled into the room.

Mere coincidence? That would be a very poor word to explain this story.

The Soldier in the Forest

C limbing a trail up into the Pyrenees in search of
somewhere to practise my archery, I stumbled
upon an encampment of French soldiers. The soldiers
all stared at me, but I pretended to have seen nothing
(well, we are all of us a little paranoid about being mis-
taken for spies ...) and walked on.

I found the ideal spot, did my preparatory breathing
exercises, and then I noticed an armoured vehicle
approaching.

I immediately went on the defensive and armed
myself with answers for any questions I might be
asked: I have a licence to use a bow, the place is perfectly safe, any objections are the business of the forest
rangers, not the army, etc. However, a colonel jumped
out of the vehicle, asked if I was a writer, and told me a
few interesting facts about the region.

Then, overcoming his almost visible shyness, he
went on to say that he, too, had written a book and
explained the unusual way it had come about.

He and his wife used to sponsor a child with lep-
rosy, and that child, who originally lived in India, was
later transferred to France. One day, feeling curious to
meet the little girl, they went to the convent where she
was being cared for by nuns. They spent a lovely afternoon, and at the end, one of the nuns asked if he would

consider helping in the spiritual education of the group of children living there. Jean Paul Sétau (the name of the colonel) explained that he had no experience of giving catechism classes, but that he would give the matter some thought and ask God what to do.

That night, after his prayers, he heard the reply: 'Instead of merely giving answers, try to find out what questions children want to ask.'

After that, Sétau had the idea of visiting several schools and asking pupils to write down everything they would like to know about life. He asked for the questions in writing, so that the shyer children would not be afraid of asking too. The results were collected together in a book – *L'Enfant qui posait toujours des questions* (*The Child Who Was Always Asking Questions*).

Here are some of those questions:

Where do we go after we die?
Why are we afraid of foreigners?
Do Martians and extraterrestrial beings really exist?
Why do accidents happen even to people who believe in God?
What does God mean?
Why are we born if we all die in the end?
How many stars are there in the sky?
Who invented war and happiness?
Does God also listen to people who don't believe in the same (Catholic) God?
Why are there poor people and ill people?
Why did God create mosquitoes and flies?
Why isn't our guardian angel beside us when we're sad?
Why do we love some people and hate others?
Who named the different colours?

If God is in Heaven and my mother is there too because she died, how come He's alive?

I hope some teachers, if they read this, will be encouraged to do the same thing. Instead of trying to impose our adult understanding of the universe, we might be reminded of some of our own, as yet unanswered, childhood questions.

In a Town in Germany

'Isn't this an interesting monument?' says Robert. The late autumn sun is beginning to set. We are in a town in Germany.

'I can't see anything,' I say. 'Just an empty square.'

'The monument is beneath our feet,' Robert insists.

I look down. I see only plain slabs, all of them the same. I don't want to disappoint my friend, but I can't see anything else in the square.

Robert explains: 'It's called "The Invisible Monument". Carved on the underneath of each of these stones is the name of a place where Jews were killed. Anonymous artists created this square during the Second World War, and continued adding slabs as new places of extermination were discovered. Even if no one could see them, it would remain here as a witness, and the future would end up finding out the truth about the past.'

Meeting in the Dentsu Gallery

Three gentlemen, all immaculately dressed, appeared in my hotel in Tokyo.

'Yesterday you gave a lecture at the Dentsu Gallery,' said one of the men. 'I just happened to go to it and I arrived at the moment when you were saying that no meeting occurs by chance. Perhaps we should introduce ourselves.'

I didn't ask how they had found out where I was staying, I didn't ask anything; people who are capable of overcoming such difficulties deserve our respect. One of the men handed me some books written in Japanese calligraphy. My interpreter became very excited. The gentleman was Kazuhito Aida, the son of a great Japanese poet of whom I had never heard.

And it was precisely the mystery of synchronicity that allowed me to know, read, and to be able to share with my readers a little of the magnificent work of Mitsuo Aida (1924–91), poet and calligrapher, whose poems remind us of the importance of innocence.

Because it has lived its life intensely
the parched grass still attracts the gaze of passers-by.
The flowers merely flower,
and they do this as well as they can.
The white lily, blooming unseen in the valley,
Does not need to explain itself to anyone;
It lives merely for beauty.
Men, however, cannot accept that 'merely'.

If tomatoes wanted to be melons,
they would look completely ridiculous.
I am always amazed
that so many people are concerned
with wanting to be what they are not;
what's the point of making yourself look ridiculous?

You don't always have to pretend to be strong,
there's no need to prove all the time that everything is going well,
you shouldn't be concerned about what other people are thinking,
cry if you need to,
it's good to cry out all your tears
(because only then will you be able to smile again).

Sometimes, on TV, I see tunnels and bridges being inaugurated. Usually, a lot of celebrities and local politicians stand in a line, in the centre of which is the minister or local governor. Then a ribbon is cut, and when the people in charge of the project return to their desks, they find lots of letters expressing recognition and admiration.

The people who sweated and worked on the project, who wielded pickaxes and spades, who laboured all through the summer heat or endured the winter cold in order to finish the job, are never seen; those who did not work by the sweat of their brow always seem to come off best.

I want to be someone capable of seeing the unseen faces, of seeing those who do not seek fame or glory, who silently fulfil the role life has given them.

I want to be able to do this because the most important things, those that shape our existence, are precisely the ones that never show their faces.

Reflections on 11 September 2001

Only now, a few years on, can I write about these events. I avoided writing about it at the time, to allow everyone to think about the consequences of the attacks in their own way.

It is always very hard to accept that a tragedy can, in some way, have positive results. As we gazed in horror at what looked more like a scene from a science fiction movie – the two towers crumbling and carrying thousands of people with them as they fell – we had two immediate responses: first, a sense of impotence and terror in the face of what was happening; second, a sense that the world would never be the same again.

The world will never be the same, it's true; but, after this long period of reflection on what happened, is there still a sense that all those people died in vain? Or can something other than death, dust, and twisted steel be found beneath the rubble of the World Trade Center?

I believe that the life of every human being is, at some point, touched by tragedy. It could be the destruction of a city, the death of a child, a baseless accusation, an illness that appears without warning and brings with it permanent disability. Life is a constant risk, and anyone who forgets this will be unprepared for the challenges that fate may have in store. Whenever we come face to face with that inevitable suffering, we are forced to try and make some sense of what is happening, to overcome our fear, and set about the process of rebuilding.

The first thing we must do when confronted by suffering and insecurity is to accept them for what they are. We cannot treat these feelings as if they had nothing to do with us, or transform them into a punishment that satisfies our eternal sense of guilt. In the rubble of the World Trade Center there were people like us, who felt secure or unhappy, fulfilled or still struggling to grow, with a family waiting for them at home, or driven to despair by the loneliness of the big city. They were American, English, German, Brazilian, Japanese; people from all corners of the globe, united by the common – and mysterious – fate of finding themselves, at around nine o'clock in the morning, in the same place, a place which, for some, was pleasant and, for others, oppressive. When the two towers collapsed, not only those people died: we all died a little, and the whole world grew smaller.

When faced by a great loss, be it material, spiritual, or psychological, we need to remember the great lessons taught to us by the wise: patience, and the certainty that everything in this life is temporary. From that point of view, let us take a new look at our values. If the world is not going to be a safe place again, at least not for many years, then why not take advantage of that sudden change, and spend our days doing the things we have always wanted to do, but for which we always lacked the courage? On the morning of 11 September 2001, how many people were in the World Trade Center against their will, following a career that didn't really suit them, doing work they didn't like, simply because it was a safe job and would guarantee them enough money for a pension in their old age?

That was the great change in the world, and those who were buried beneath the rubble of the two towers are now making us rethink our own lives and values. When the towers collapsed, they dragged down with them dreams and hopes; but they also opened up our own horizons, and allowed each of us to reflect upon the meaning of our lives.

According to a story told about events immediately after the bombing of Dresden, a man was walking past a plot of land covered in rubble when he saw three workmen.

'What are you doing?' he asked.

The first workman turned round and said: 'Can't you see? I'm shifting these stones!'

'Can't you see? I'm earning a wage!' said the second workman.

'Can't you see?' said the third workman. 'I'm rebuilding the cathedral!'

Although those three workmen were all engaged on the same task, only one had a sense of the real meaning of his life and his work. Let us hope that in the world that exists after 11 September 2001, each of us will prove able to lift ourselves out from beneath our own emotional rubble and rebuild the cathedral we always dreamed of, but never dared to create.

God's Signs

Isabelita told me the following story. An old illiterate Arab used to pray with such fervour each night that the wealthy owner of the great caravan decided to summon him so as to talk to him.

'Why do you pray with such devotion? How do you know God exists when you don't even know how to read?'

'I do know, sir. I can read everything that the Great Celestial Father writes?'

'But how?'

The humble servant explained.

'When you receive a letter from someone far away, how do you recognize the writer?'

'By the handwriting.'

'When you receive a jewel, how do you know who made it?'

'By the goldsmith's mark.'

'When you hear animals moving about near the tent, how do you know if it was a sheep, a horse, or an ox?'

'By its footprints,' replied the owner, surprised at all these questions.

The old man invited him to come outside with him and showed him the sky.

'Neither the things written up there, nor the desert down below, could have been made or written by the hand of man.'

Alone on the Road

Life is like a great bicycle race, whose aim is to fulfil our personal legend, which, according to the ancient alchemists, is our true mission on earth.

We all set off together, sharing friendship and enthusiasm; but as the race progresses, that initial happiness gives way to the real challenges: tiredness, boredom, doubts about our own abilities. We notice that a few friends have, in their hearts, already given up. They are still cycling, but only because they cannot stop in the middle of the road. There are more and more of them, pedalling along beside the support vehicle – also known as routine – talking amongst themselves, fulfilling their obligations, but oblivious to the beauties and challenges of the road.

We eventually leave them behind us, and then we come face to face with loneliness, with unfamiliar bends in the road, and mechanical problems with our bicycle. At a certain stage, after suffering a few falls with no one near at hand to help, we begin to ask ourselves if it's really worth all the effort.

Yes, it is. It's just a question of not giving up. Father Alan Jones says that in order to overcome these obstacles, we need four invisible forces: love, death, power and time.

We must love because we ourselves are loved by God.

We must have an awareness of death in order fully to understand life.

We must struggle in order to grow, but without allowing ourselves to be deceived by the power that is gained through that struggle, because we know that such power is worthless.

Finally, we must accept that our soul – even though it is eternal – is at this moment caught in the web of time, with all its opportunities and limitations.

Therefore, on our solitary bicycle race, we must behave as if time existed and do everything we can to value each second, to rest when necessary, but to keep cycling towards the divine light, and not be put off by any moments of anxiety.

These four forces cannot be treated as problems to be solved, because they are beyond anyone's control. We must accept them, and let them teach us what we need to learn.

We live in a universe that is at once vast enough to enclose us, and small enough to fit inside our heart. In the soul of man is the soul of the world, the silence of wisdom. As we pedal towards our goal, we must make a point of asking ourselves: 'What is beautiful about today?' The sun might be shining, but if it happens to be raining, always remember that this only means that the dark clouds will soon have disappeared. The clouds do disappear; but the sun remains the same, and never goes away. In moments of loneliness, it is important to remember this.

When things get hard, let us not forget that – independent of race, colour, social situation, beliefs, or culture – everyone has experienced exactly the same. A

lovely prayer written by the Egyptian Sufi master Dhu
'l-Nun (d. AD 861) neatly sums up the attitude one
needs to adopt at such times:

O God, when I listen to the voices of the animals, to
the sound of the trees, the murmur of the water, the
singing of the birds, to the rushing of the wind or to
the rumble of thunder, I see in them evidence of
Your unity; I feel that You are supreme power,
supreme knowledge, supreme wisdom, supreme
justice.

O God, I also recognize you in the difficulties I
am experiencing now. God, let Your satisfaction be
my satisfaction, and let me be Your joy, the joy that
a Father takes in his child. And let me remember
You with calmness and determination, even when it
is hard for me to say: I love You.

The Funny Thing About Human Beings

A man asked my friend Jaime Cohen: 'What is the human being's funniest characteristic?'

Cohen said: 'Our contradictoriness. We are in such a hurry to grow up, and then we long for our lost childhood. We make ourselves ill earning money, and then spend all our money on getting well again. We think so much about the future that we neglect the present, and thus experience neither the present nor the future. We live as if we were never going to die, and die as if we had never lived.'

An Around-the-World Trip After Death

I have often thought about what happens as we scatter little bits of ourselves around the world. I have cut my hair in Tokyo, trimmed my nails in Norway, and spilled my own blood on a mountain in France. In my first book, *The Archives of Hell*, I speculated briefly on this subject, about whether we had to sow a little of our own body in various parts of the world so that, in a future life, we would be sure to find something familiar. Recently, I read in the French newspaper *Le Figaro* an article by Guy Barret about a real-life event in June 2001 when someone took this idea to its ultimate consequences.

The article was about an American woman, Vera Anderson, who spent all her life in Medford, Oregon. When she was getting on in years, she suffered a stroke, aggravated by pulmonary emphysema, which forced her to spend years confined to her room, connected up to an oxygen machine. This was, in itself, a torment, but in Vera's case, it was even more of one, because she had always dreamed of travelling the world, and had saved up her money in order to be able to do so when she retired.

Vera managed to move to Colorado so that she could spend the rest of her days with her son, Ross.

There, before making her final journey – the one from which we never return – she made a decision. She might not have been able to travel even in her own country while alive, but she would travel the world after her death.

Ross went to the local notary public and registered his mother's will. When she died, she would like to be cremated. Nothing unusual about that. But the will went on to stipulate that her ashes were to be placed in 241 small bags, which were to be sent to the heads of postal services in the 50 American states, and to each of the 191 countries of the world, so that at least part of her body would end up visiting the places she had always dreamed about.

As soon as Vera died, Ross carried out her last wishes with all the respect one could hope for in a son. With each remittance, he enclosed a brief letter in which he asked that his mother be given a decent funeral.

Everyone who received Vera Anderson's ashes treated Ross's request with utter seriousness. In the four corners of the earth, a silent chain of solidarity was formed, in which sympathetic strangers organized the most diverse of ceremonies, depending on the place that the late Mrs Anderson would have liked to visit.

Thus Vera's ashes were scattered in Lake Titicaca, in Bolivia, according to the ancient traditions of the Aymara Indians; they were scattered on the river in front of the royal palace in Stockholm; on the banks of the Chao Phraya in Thailand; in a Shinto temple in Japan; on the glaciers of Antarctica; and in the Sahara desert. The sisters of charity in an orphanage in South America (the article does not specify in which country) prayed for a week before scattering the ashes in the garden, and then decided that Vera Anderson should be considered a kind of guardian angel of the place.

Ross Anderson received photos from the five continents, from all races and all cultures, showing men and women honouring his mother's last wishes. When we see today's divided world, a world in which no one seems to care about anyone else, Vera Anderson's last journey fills us with hope, for it shows us that there is still respect, love and generosity in the souls of our fellow human beings, however far away they may be.

Who Would Like This Twenty-Dollar Bill?

Cassan Said Amer tells the story of a lecturer who began a seminar by holding up a twenty-dollar bill and asking: 'Who would like this twenty-dollar bill?'

Several hands went up, but the lecturer said: 'Before I give it to you, I have to do something.'

He screwed it up into a ball and said: 'Who still wants this bill?'

The hands went up again.

'And what if I do this to it?'

He threw the crumpled bill at the wall, dropped it on the floor, insulted it, trampled on it, and once more showed them the bill – now all creased and dirty. He repeated the question, and the hands stayed up.

'Never forget this scene,' he said. 'It doesn't matter what I do to this money. It is still a twenty-dollar bill. So often in our lives, we are crumpled, trampled, ill-treated, insulted, and yet, despite all that, we are still worth the same.'

The Two Jewels

From the Cistercian monk, Marcos Garria, in Burgos, in Spain.

'Sometimes God withdraws a particular blessing from someone so that the person can comprehend Him as something other than a being of whom one asks favours and makes requests. He knows how far He can test a soul, and never goes beyond that point. At such moments, we must never say: "God has abandoned me." He will never do that, even though we may sometimes abandon Him. If the Lord sets us a great test, he always gives us sufficient – I would say more than sufficient – grace to pass that test.'

In this regard, one of my readers, Camila Galvão Piva, sent me an interesting story, entitled 'The Two Jewels'.

A very devout rabbi lived happily with his family – an admirable wife and their two beloved sons. Once, because of his work, the rabbi had to be away from home for several days. During that period, both children were killed in a terrible car accident.

Alone, the mother suffered in silence. However, because she was a strong woman, sustained by faith and trust in God, she endured the shock with dignity and courage. But how was she to break the tragic news to her husband? His faith was equally strong, but he had, in the past, been taken into hospital with heart problems, and his wife feared that finding out about the tragedy might cause his death too.

All she could do was to pray to God to advise her on the best way to act. On the eve of her husband's return, she prayed hard and was granted the grace of an answer.

The following day, the rabbi arrived home, embraced his wife, and asked after the children. The woman told him not to worry about them now, but to take a bath and rest.

Some time later, they sat down to lunch. She asked him all about his trip, and he told her everything that had happened to him; he spoke about God's mercy, and then again asked about the children.

The wife, somewhat awkwardly, replied: 'Don't worry about the children. We'll deal with them later. First, I need your help to solve what I consider to be a very grave problem.'

Her husband asked anxiously: 'What's happened? I thought you looked distressed. Tell me everything that is on your mind, and I'm sure that, with God's help, we can solve any problem together.'

'While you were away, a friend of ours visited us and left two jewels of incalculable value here for me to look after. They're really lovely jewels! I've never seen anything so beautiful before. He has since come to claim them back, and I don't want to return them. I've grown too fond of them. What should I do?'

'I can't understand your behaviour at all! You've never been a woman given to vanity!'

'It's just that I've never seen such jewels before! I can't bear the idea of losing them forever.'

And the rabbi said firmly: 'No one can lose something he or she has not possessed. Keeping those jewels would be tantamount to stealing them. We will give them back, and I will help you make up for their loss. We will do this together today.'

'As you wish, my love. The treasures will be returned. In fact, they already have been. The two precious jewels were our sons. God entrusted them to our care, and while you were away, he came to fetch them back. They have gone.'

The rabbi understood. He embraced his wife, and together they wept many tears; but he had understood the message and, from that day on, they struggled to bear their loss together.

Self-Deception

I t is part of human nature always to judge others very severely and, when the wind turns against us, always to find an excuse for our own misdeeds, or to blame someone else for our mistakes. The story that follows illustrates what I mean.

A messenger was sent on an urgent mission to a distant city. He saddled up his horse and set off at a gallop. After passing several inns where animals like him were normally fed, the horse thought: 'We're not stopping to eat at any stables, which means that I'm being treated, not like a horse, but like a human being. Like all other men, I will eat in the next big city we reach.'

But the big cities all passed by, one after the other, and his rider continued on his way. The horse began to think: 'Perhaps I haven't been changed into a human being after all, but into an angel, because angels have no need to eat.'

Finally, they reached their destination and the animal was led to the stable, where he greedily devoured the hay he found there.

'Why believe that things have changed simply because they do not happen quite as expected?' he said to himself. 'I'm not a man or an angel. I'm simply a hungry horse.'

The Art of Trying

Pablo Picasso said: 'God is, above all, an artist. He invented the giraffe, the elephant, and the ant. He never tried to follow one particular style. He simply kept on doing whatever he felt like doing.'

It is the desire to walk that creates the path ahead; however, when we set off on the journey towards our dream, we feel very afraid, as if we had to get everything right first time. But, given that we all live different lives, who decided what 'getting everything right' means? If God made the giraffe, the elephant, and the ant, and we are trying to live in His image, why do we have to follow any other model? A model might sometimes help us to avoid repeating the stupid mistakes that others have made, but, more often than not, it becomes a prison that makes us repeat what everyone else has always done.

It means making sure your tie always matches your socks. It means being forced to have the same opinions tomorrow as you had today. Where does that leave the constantly shifting world?

As long as it doesn't harm anyone, change your opinions now and then and be unashamedly contradictory. You have that right; it doesn't matter what other people think, because they're going to think something anyway.

When we decide to act, some excesses may occur. An old culinary adage says: 'You can't make an omelette without breaking eggs.' It's also natural that unexpected conflicts should arise, and it's natural that wounds may be inflicted during those conflicts. The wounds pass, and only the scars remain.

This is a blessing. These scars stay with us throughout our life and are very helpful. If, at some point – simply because it would make life easier, or for whatever other reason – the desire to return to the past becomes very great, we need only look at those scars. They are the marks left by the handcuffs, and will remind us of the horrors of prison, and we will keep walking straight ahead.

So, relax. Let the universe move around you and discover the joy of surprising yourself. 'God has chosen the foolish things of the world to confound the wise,' says St Paul.

A warrior of light often finds that certain moments repeat themselves. He is often faced by the same problems and situations and, seeing these difficult situations return, he grows depressed, thinking that he is incapable of making any progress in life.

'I've been through all this before,' he says to his heart.

'Yes, you have been through all this before,' replies his heart. 'But you have never been beyond it.'

Then the warrior realizes that these repeated experiences have but one aim: to teach him what he has not yet learned. He always finds a different solution for each repeated battle, and he does not consider his failures to be mistakes but, rather, as steps along the path to a meeting with himself.

The Dangers Besetting the Spiritual Search

As people start to pay more attention to the things of the spirit, another phenomenon occurs: a feeling of intolerance towards the spiritual search of others. Every day, I receive magazines, e-mails, letters, and pamphlets, trying to prove that one path is better than another, and containing a whole series of rules to follow in order to achieve 'enlightenment'. Given the growing volume of such correspondence, I have decided to write a little about what I consider to be the dangers of this search.

Myth 1: The mind can cure everything

This is not true, and I prefer to illustrate this particular myth with a story. Some years ago, a friend of mine – deeply involved in the spiritual search – began to feel feverish and ill. She spent the whole night trying to 'mentalize' her body, using all the techniques she knew, in order to cure herself purely with the power of the mind. The following day, her children, who were getting worried, urged her to go to the doctor, but she refused, saying that she was 'purifying' her spirit. Only when the situation became untenable did she agree to go to the hospital, where she had to have an emergency operation for appendicitis. So, be very careful: it's better sometimes to ask God to guide your doctor's hands than to try to cure yourself alone.

Myth 2: Red meat drives away the divine light

Obviously, if you belong to a certain religion, you will have to respect established rules – Jews and Muslims, for example, do not eat pork, and, in their case, this practice forms part of their faith. However, the world is being flooded with a wave of 'purification through food'. Radical vegetarians look at people who eat meat as if they had murdered the animal themselves; but, then, aren't plants living things too? Nature is a constant cycle of life and death and, one day, we will be the ones going back into the earth to feed it. So if you don't belong to a religion that forbids certain foods, eat whatever your organism needs.

I would like to tell a story about the Russian magus Gurdjieff. When he was young, he went to visit a great teacher and, in order to impress him, he ate only vegetables. One night, the teacher asked him why he kept to such a strict diet. Gurdjieff replied: 'In order to keep my body clean.' The teacher laughed and advised him to stop this practice at once. If he continued, he would end up like a hothouse flower – very pure, but incapable of withstanding the challenges of travelling and of life. As Jesus said: 'It is not what goes into the mouth that defiles a man, but what comes out of the mouth.'

Myth 3: God is sacrifice

Many people seek the path of sacrifice and self-immo-lation, stating that we must suffer in this world in order to find happiness in the next. Now, if this world is a blessing from God, why not try to enjoy to the full the delights that life offers us? We are very accustomed to the image of Christ nailed to the Cross; but we forget that his Passion lasted only three days. The rest of the time he spent travelling, meeting people, eating, drink-ing, and preaching his message of tolerance, so much so that his first miracle was, in a sense, 'politically incorrect', for when the wine ran out at the Cana wed-ding, he turned the water into wine. He did this, I believe, to demonstrate to us all that there is nothing wrong with being happy, enjoying yourself, joining in with the party, because God is much closer to us when we are with others. Mohammed said: 'If we are un-happy, we bring unhappiness upon our friends also.' Buddha, after a long period of trial and renunciation, was so weak that he almost drowned; when he was res-cued by a shepherd, he understood that isolation and sacrifice distance us from the miracle of life.

Myth 4: There is only one path to God

This is the most dangerous of all the myths, for from it spring all the many explanations of the Great Mystery, as well as religious strife and our tendency to judge our fellow men and women. We can choose a religion (I, for example, am Catholic), but we must understand that if our brother chooses a different religion, he will eventually reach the same point of light that we are seeking in our spiritual practices. Finally, it is worth remembering that we cannot shift responsibility for our decisions onto priest, rabbi, or imam. We are the ones who build the road to paradise with each and every one of our actions.

My Father-in-Law, Christiano Oiticica

Shortly before he died, my father-in-law summoned his family.

'I know that death is only a journey, and I want to make that voyage without sadness. So that you won't worry, I will send you a sign that it really is worthwhile helping others in this life.'

He asked to be cremated and for his ashes to be scattered over Arpoador Beach while a tape recorder played his favourite music.

He died two days later. A friend arranged the cremation in São Paulo and, once back in Rio, we went straight to the beach armed with a tape recorder, tapes, and the package containing the cremation urn. When we reached the sea, we discovered that the lid of the urn was firmly screwed down. We tried in vain to open it.

The only other person around was a beggar, and he came over to us and asked: 'What's the problem?'

My brother-in-law said: 'We need a screwdriver so that we can get at my father's ashes inside this urn.'

'Well, he must have been a very good man, because I've just found this,' said the beggar.

And he held out a screwdriver.

Thank You, President Bush*

Thank you, great leader George W. Bush.

Thank you for showing everyone what a danger Saddam Hussein represents. Many of us might otherwise have forgotten that he had used chemical weapons against his own people, against the Kurds, and against the Iranians. Hussein is a bloodthirsty dictator, and one of the clearest expressions of evil in today's world.

But this is not my only reason for thanking you. During the first two months of 2003, you have shown the world a great many other important things and, therefore, deserve my gratitude.

So, remembering a poem I learned as a child, I want to say thank you.

Thank you for showing everyone that the Turkish people and their parliament are not for sale, not even for 26 billion dollars.

Thank you for revealing to the world the gulf that exists between the decisions made by those in power

---

* This article was first published on an English website on 8 March 2003, two weeks before the invasion of Iraq. During that month, it was the most widely published article about the war, and had a readership of about 500 million.

and the wishes of the people. Thank you for making it clear that neither José María Aznar nor Tony Blair give the slightest weight to, or show the slightest respect for, the votes they received. Aznar is perfectly capable of ignoring the fact that 90 per cent of Spaniards are against the war, and Blair is unmoved by the largest public demonstration to take place in Britain in the last thirty years.

Thank you for making it necessary for Tony Blair to go to the British Parliament with a fabricated dossier written by a student ten years ago and present this as 'damning evidence collected by the British Secret Service'.

Thank you for sending Colin Powell to the UN Security Council with proof and photographs, thus allowing for these to be publicly refuted one week later by Hans Blix, the Inspector responsible for disarming Iraq.

Thank you for adopting your current position, thus ensuring that, at the plenary session, the anti-war speech of the French Foreign Minister, Dominique de Villepin, was greeted with applause – something, as far as I know, that has only happened once before in the history of the UN, on the occasion of a speech by Nelson Mandela.

Thank you, too, because, after all your efforts to promote war, the normally divided Arab nations, at their meeting in Cairo during the last week in February, were, for the first time, unanimous in their condemnation of any invasion.

Thank you for your rhetoric stating that 'the UN now has a chance to demonstrate its relevance', a statement that made even the most reluctant countries take up a position opposing any attack on Iraq.

Thank you for your foreign policy, which provoked the British Foreign Secretary, Jack Straw, into declaring that, in the twenty-first century, 'a war can have a moral justification', thus causing him to lose all credibility.

Thank you for trying to divide a Europe that is currently struggling for unification. This was a warning that will not go unheeded.

Thank you for having achieved something that very few have so far managed to do in this century: the bringing together of millions of people on all continents to fight for the same idea, even though that idea is opposed to yours.

Thank you for making us feel once more that, though our words may not be heard, they are at least spoken. This will make us stronger in the future.

Thank you for ignoring us, for marginalizing all those who oppose your decision, because the future of the earth belongs to the excluded.

Thank you, because, without you, we would not have realized our own ability to mobilize. It may serve no purpose this time, but it will doubtless be useful later on.

Now that there seems no way of silencing the drums of war, I would like to say, as an ancient European king said to an invader: 'May your morning be a beautiful one, and may the sun shine on your soldiers' armour, for in the afternoon, I will defeat you.'

Thank you for allowing us – an army of anonymous people filling the streets in an attempt to stop a process that is already underway – to know what it feels like to be powerless, and to learn to grapple with that feeling and transform it.

So, enjoy your morning and whatever glory it may yet bring you.

Thank you for not listening to us, and for not taking us seriously; but know that we are listening to you, and that we will not forget your words.

Thank you, great leader, George W. Bush.

Thank you very much.

The Intelligent Clerk

At an airbase in Africa, the writer Antoine de Saint-Exupéry made a collection amongst his friends to help a Moroccan clerk who wanted to go back to the city of his birth. He managed to collect one thousand francs.

One of the pilots flew the clerk to Casablanca, and when he returned, he described what had happened.

'As soon as he arrived, he went out to supper in the best restaurant, gave lavish tips, ordered drinks all round, and bought dolls for the children in his village. The man had absolutely no idea when it came to looking after his money.'

'On the contrary,' said Saint-Exupéry, 'he knew that people are the best investment in the world. By spending freely like that, he managed to regain the respect of his fellow villagers, who will probably end up giving him a job. After all, only a conqueror can be that generous.'

The Third Passion

During the last fifteen years, I have had three consuming passions, of the kind where you read everything you can find on the subject, talk obsessively about it, seek out people who share your enthusiasm, and fall asleep and wake up thinking about it. The first was when I bought a computer. I abandoned the typewriter for ever, and discovered the freedom this gave me (I am writing this in a small French town, using a machine that weighs just over three pounds, contains ten years of my professional life, and on which I can find whatever I need in less than five seconds). The second was when I first used the internet, which, even then, was already a larger repository of knowledge than the very largest of conventional libraries.

The third passion, however, has nothing to do with technological advances. It is … the bow and arrow. In my youth, I read a fascinating book entitled *Zen in the Art of Archery* by Eugen Herrigel, in which he described his spiritual journey through the practice of that sport. The idea stayed in my subconscious until, one day, in the Pyrenees, I met an archer. We chatted away, he lent me a bow and some arrows, and, ever since, I have hardly let a day go by without practising shooting at a target.

At home, in my apartment in Brazil, I set up my own target (the sort you can take down in a matter of minutes when visitors come). In the French mountains, I practise outside every day, and this has so far landed me in bed twice – with hypothermia, after spending more than two hours in temperatures of –6°C. I could only take part in the World Economic Forum this year in Davos thanks to powerful painkillers: two days before, I had caused a painful muscle inflammation just by holding my arm in the wrong position.

And where does the fascination lie? Being able to shoot at targets with a bow and arrow (a weapon that dates back to 30,000 BC) has no practical application. But Eugen Herrigel, who first awoke this passion in me, knew what he was talking about. Below are some extracts from *Zen in the Art of Archery* (which can be applied to various activities in daily life).

When you apply tension, focus it solely on the thing that you require the tension for; otherwise, conserve your energies, learn (with the bow) that in order to achieve something, you do not need to take a giant step, but simply to focus on your objective.

My teacher gave me a very stiff bow. I asked why he was starting to teach me as if I were a professional. He replied: 'If you begin with easy things, it leaves you unprepared for the great challenges. It's best to know at once what difficulties you are likely to meet on the road.'

For a long time, I could not draw the bow correctly, until, one day, my teacher showed me a breathing exercise, and it suddenly became easy. I asked why he had taken such a long time to correct me. He replied: 'If I had shown you the breathing exercises right from the start, you would have thought them unnecessary. Now you will believe what I say and will practise as if it were really important. That is what good teachers do.'

Releasing the arrow happens instinctively, but first you must have an intimate knowledge of the bow, the arrow and the target. When it comes to life's challenges, making the perfect move also involves intuition; however, we can only forget technique once we have mastered it completely.

After four years, when I had mastered the bow, my teacher congratulated me. I felt pleased and said that I was now halfway along the road. 'No,' said my teacher. 'To avoid falling into treacherous traps, it is best to consider that you have covered half your journey only when you have walked ninety percent of the road.'*

* Note: using bows and arrows can be dangerous. In some countries (such as France) the bow is classified as a weapon, and archery can only be practised if you have the necessary license and only in expressly authorized places.

The Catholic and the Muslim

I was talking to a Catholic priest and a young Muslim man over lunch. When the waiter came by with a tray, we all helped ourselves, except the Muslim, who was keeping the annual fast prescribed by the Koran.

When lunch was over, and people were leaving, one of the other guests couldn't resist saying: 'You see how fanatical these Muslims are! I'm glad to see you Catholics aren't like them.'

'But we are,' said the priest. 'He is trying to serve God just as I am. We merely follow different laws.' And he concluded: 'It's a shame that people see only the differences that separate them. If you were to look with more love, you would mainly see what we have in common, then half the world's problems would be solved.'

Evil Wants Good to Prevail

One day, the Persian poet, Rumi que Mo'avia, the first of the Ommiad caliphs, was sleeping in his palace when he was woken up by a strange man.

'Who are you?' he asked.

'I am Lucifer,' came the reply.

'And what do you want?'

'It is the hour for prayers, and yet you are still asleep.'

Mo'avia was amazed. Why was the Prince of Darkness, who seeks out the souls of men of little faith, reminding him to fulfil his religious duties?

'Remember,' Lucifer explained, 'I was brought up as an angel of light. Despite everything that has happened to me, I cannot forget my origins. A man may travel to Rome or to Jerusalem, but he always carries the values of his own country in his heart. Well, the same thing happens with me. I still love the Creator, who nourished me when I was young and taught me to do good. When I rebelled against Him, it was not because I did not love Him; on the contrary, I loved Him so much that I felt jealous when He created Adam. At that moment, I wanted to defy the Lord, and that was my downfall; nevertheless, I still remember the blessings bestowed on me and hope that, perhaps, by doing good, I can one day return to paradise.'

Mo'avia replied: 'I can't believe what you're saying. You have been responsible for the destruction of many people on earth.'

'Well, you *should* believe it,' insisted Lucifer. 'Only God can build and destroy, because He is all-powerful. When He created man, He also created, as part of life, desire, vengeance, compassion, and fear. So when you look at the evil around you, don't blame me; I merely reflect back the bad things that happen.'

Mo'avia was sure that something was wrong, and he began to pray desperately to God to enlighten him. He spent the whole night talking and arguing with Lucifer; but despite the brilliant arguments he heard, he remained unconvinced.

When day was dawning, Lucifer finally gave in and said:

'You're right. When I came yesterday to wake you up so that you would not miss the hour of prayer, my intention was not to bring you closer to the Divine Light. I knew that if you failed to fulfil your obligations, you would feel profoundly sad and, over the next few days, would pray with twice the faith, asking forgiveness for having forgotten the correct ritual. In the eyes of God, each one of those prayers made with love and repentance would be equivalent to two hundred prayers said in an ordinary, automatic way. You would end up more purified and more inspired; God would love you more; and I would be still further from your soul.'

Lucifer vanished, and an angel of light took his place:

'Never forget today's lesson,' the angel said to Mo'avia. 'Sometimes evil comes disguised as an emissary of good, but its real intention is to cause more destruction.'

On that day, and the days that followed, Mo'avia prayed with repentance, compassion, and faith. His prayers were heard a thousand times by God.

The Law of Jante

'What do you think of Princess Martha-Louise?'
The Norwegian journalist was interviewing me on the shores of Lake Geneva. Now, generally speaking, I refuse to answer questions that are unrelated to my work, but there was, in this case, a motive behind his curiosity: the princess had had the names of various people who had been important in her life embroidered on a dress she wore for her thirtieth birthday – and mine was amongst those names (my wife thought it such a good idea that she decided to do the same for her fiftieth birthday, adding the credit 'inspired by the Princess of Norway' in one corner).

'I think she is a sensitive, courteous, intelligent person,' I replied. 'I was fortunate enough to meet her in Oslo, where she introduced me to her husband, who, like myself, is a writer.'

I paused, but then decided to continue.

'There's one thing I don't understand: why has the Norwegian press started attacking his literary work now that he's the princess's husband? Before, he used to get very positive reviews.'

This was not really a question, more a provocation, because I could already imagine what the reply would be. The reason the reviews had changed was envy, that most bitter of human emotions.

The journalist, however, was more sophisticated than that.

'Because he broke the Law of Jante.'

Since I had clearly never heard of this law, he explained what it was. As I continued my journey, I came to realize that it was, indeed, hard to find anyone in the Scandinavian countries who had not heard of the law. It may have existed since the beginning of civilization, but it was only officially set down in written form in 1933 by the writer Aksel Sandemose in his novel *A Fugitive Crossing His Tracks*.

The sad fact is that the Law of Jante doesn't only exist in Scandinavia. It is a rule that applies all over the world, however much Brazilians may say: 'This could only happen here', and the French may affirm: 'That's just the way it is in France'. Since the reader must, by now, be getting irritated – having read half of this and still having no clear idea what this Law of Jante is – I will try to summarize it here, in my own words: 'You are worthless; no one is interested in what you think, therefore you had better opt for mediocrity and anonymity. Do this, and you will never face any major problems in life.'

The Law of Jante puts into context the feelings of jealousy and envy that can prove so problematic to people like Princess Martha-Louise's husband, Ari Behn. That is just one negative aspect of the law. There is, however, another far more dangerous one.

It is thanks to this law that the world has been manipulated in all kinds of ways by people who are not afraid of what others might say, and who often end up achieving their own evil ends. We have just been witness to a pointless war in Iraq, which continues to cost many lives; we see the great gap that exists between rich countries and poor; everywhere we see social injustice, rampant violence, people forced to give up their dreams because of unwarranted and cowardly attacks. Before starting the Second World War, Hitler signalled his intentions in various ways, and what made him continue with his plans regardless was the knowledge that no one would dare to challenge him – because of the Law of Jante.

Mediocrity can be very comfortable until, one day, tragedy knocks on the door, and then people wonder: 'But why didn't anyone say anything, when everyone could see this was going to happen?'

Simple: no one said anything because *they* didn't say anything either.

Therefore, in order to prevent things from getting even worse, perhaps it is time that an Anti-Law of Jante was written: 'You are worth much more than you think. Your work and your presence on this earth are important, even though you may not believe it. Of course, such ideas could land you in a lot of trouble for breaking the Law of Jante, but don't be intimidated. Continue to live without fear, and you will triumph in the end.'

The Old Lady in Copacabana

She was standing in the pedestrian precinct on Avenida Atlântica, with a guitar and a handwritten notice: 'Let's sing together.'

She started playing on her own. Then a drunk arrived and another old lady, and they started singing with her. Soon a small crowd was singing, and another small crowd provided the audience, applauding at the end of each song.

'Why do you do this?' I asked her, between songs.

'So as not to be alone,' she said. 'My life is very lonely, as it is for nearly all old people.'

If only everyone solved their problems like that.

Remaining Open to Love

There are times when we long to be able to help someone whom we love very much, but we can do nothing. Circumstances will not allow us to approach them, or the person is closed off to any gesture of solidarity and support.

Then all we are left with is love. At such times, when we can do nothing else, we can still love – without expecting any reward or change or gratitude.

If we do this, the energy of love will begin to transform the universe about us. Wherever this energy appears, it always achieves its ends. 'Time does not transform man. Will-power does not transform man. Love transforms,' says Henry Drummond.

I read in the newspaper about a little girl in Brasília who was brutally beaten by her parents. As a result, she lost all physical movement, as well as the ability to speak.

Once admitted to hospital, she was cared for by a nurse who said to her every day: 'I love you.' Although the doctors assured her that the child could not hear and that all her efforts were in vain, the nurse continued to say: 'Don't forget, I love you.'

Three weeks later, the child recovered the power of movement. Four weeks later, she could again talk and smile. The nurse never gave any interviews, and the newspaper did not publish her name, but let me set this down here, so that we never forget: love cures.

Love transforms and love cures; but, sometimes, love builds deadly traps and can end up destroying a person who had resolved to give him or herself completely. What is this complex feeling which, deep down, is the only reason we continue to live, struggle and improve?

It would be irresponsible of me to attempt to define it, because I, along with every other human being, can only feel it. Thousands of books have been written on the subject, plays have been put on, films produced, poems composed, sculptures carved out of wood or marble; and yet all any artist can convey is the idea of a feeling, not the feeling itself.

But I have learned that this feeling is present in the small things, and manifests itself in the most insignificant of our actions. It is necessary, therefore, to keep love always in mind, regardless of whether or not we take action.

Picking up the phone and saying the affectionate words we have been postponing. Opening the door to someone who needs our help. Accepting a job. Leaving a job. Taking a decision that we were putting off for later. Asking forgiveness for a mistake we made and which keeps niggling at us. Demanding a right that is ours. Opening an account at the local florist's, which is a far more important shop than the jeweller's. Putting music on really loud when the person you love is far away, and turning the volume down when he or she is near. Knowing when to say 'yes' and 'no', because love works with all our energies. Discovering a sport that can be played by two. Not following any recipe, not even those contained in this paragraph, because love requires creativity.

And when none of this is possible, when all that remains is loneliness, then remember this story that a reader once sent to me.

A rose dreamed day and night about bees, but no bee ever landed on her petals.

The flower, however, continued to dream. During the long nights, she imagined a heaven full of bees, which flew down to bestow fond kisses on her. By doing this, she was able to last until the next day, when she opened again to the light of the sun.

One night, the moon, who knew of the rose's loneliness, asked: 'Aren't you tired of waiting?'

'Possibly, but I have to keep trying.'

'Why?'

'Because if I don't remain open, I will simply fade away.'

At times, when loneliness seems to crush all beauty, the only way to resist is to remain open.

Believing in the Impossible

William Blake said: 'What is now proved was once only imagined.' And because of this we have the airplane, space flights, and the computer on which I am writing this. In Lewis Carroll's masterpiece *Alice Through the Looking Glass*, there is a dialogue between Alice and the White Queen, who has just said something utterly unbelievable.

> 'I can't believe *that*!' said Alice.
>
> 'Can't you?' the Queen said in a pitying tone. 'Try again: draw a long breath, and shut your eyes.'
>
> Alice laughed. 'There's no use trying,' she said: 'one *can't* believe impossible things.'
>
> 'I daresay you haven't had much practice,' said the Queen. 'When I was your age, I always did it for half-an-hour a day. Why, sometimes, I've believed as many as six impossible things before breakfast.'

Life is constantly telling us: 'Believe!' Believing that a miracle could happen at any moment is necessary for our happiness, but also for our protection and to justify our existence. In today's world, many people think it is impossible to do away with poverty, to bring about a just society, and to lessen the religious tension that appears to be growing with each day.

Most people avoid the struggle for the most diverse of reasons: conformism, age, a sense of the ridiculous, a feeling of impotence. We see our fellow human beings being treated unjustly and we say nothing. 'I'm not going to get involved in fights unnecessarily' is the excuse given.

This is the attitude of the coward. Anyone travelling a spiritual path carries with him a code of honour that must be obeyed. A voice crying out against wrongdoing is always heard by God.

Even so, sometimes we hear the following remark: 'I live my life believing in dreams, and I often do my best to combat injustice, but I always end up disappointed.'

A warrior of light knows that certain impossible battles nevertheless deserve to be fought, which is why he is not afraid of disappointments, for he knows the power of his sword and the strength of his love. He vehemently rejects those who are incapable of taking decisions and are always trying to shift responsibility for all the bad things that happen in the world onto someone else.

If he does not struggle against what is wrong – even if it seems beyond his strength – he will never find the right road.

Arash Hejazi once sent me the following note: 'Today, I got caught in a heavy shower while walking along the street. Fortunately, I had my umbrella and my rain-cape; however, both were in the boot of my car, which was parked some way away. While I was running to get them, I thought about the strange signal I was receiving from God: we always have the necessary resources to face the storms that life throws at us, but most of the time, those resources are locked up in the depths of our heart, and we waste an enormous amount of time trying to find them. By the time we've found them, we have already been defeated by adversity.'

Let us, therefore, always be prepared; otherwise, we either miss an opportunity or lose the battle.

The Storm Approaches

I know that a storm is coming because I can look far into the distance and see what is happening on the horizon. Of course, the light helps – the sun is setting, and that always emphasizes the shapes of the clouds. I can see flickers of lightning, too.

There is not a sound to be heard. The wind is blowing neither more nor less strongly than before, but I know there is going to be a storm because I am used to studying the horizon.

I stop walking. There is nothing more exciting or more terrifying than watching a storm approach. My first thought is to seek shelter, but that could prove dangerous. A shelter can turn out to be a trap – soon the wind will start to blow and will be strong enough to tear off roof tiles, break branches and bring down electricity lines.

I remember an old friend of mine who lived in Normandy as a child and who witnessed the Allied landing in Nazi-occupied France. I'll never forget his words: 'I woke up, and the horizon was full of warships. On the beach beside my house, the German soldiers were watching the same scene, but what terrified me most was the silence. The total silence that precedes a life-or-death struggle.'

It is that same silence that surrounds me now, and which is gradually being replaced by the sound – very soft – of the breeze in the maize fields around me. The atmospheric pressure is changing. The storm is getting closer and closer, and the silence is beginning to give way to the gentle rustling of leaves.

I have witnessed many storms in my life. Most storms have taken me by surprise, and so I've had to learn – and very quickly too – to look farther off, to understand that I cannot control the weather, to practise the art of patience, and to respect nature's fury. Things do not always happen the way I would have wanted, and it's best that I get used to that.

Many years ago, I wrote a song that said: 'I lost my fear of the rain because when the rain falls to earth it always brings with it something of the air'. It's best to master my fear, to be worthy of the words I wrote, and to understand that, however bad the storm, it will eventually pass.

The wind has begun to blow harder. I am in open countryside and there are trees on the horizon that, at least in theory, will attract the lightning. My skin is waterproof, even if my clothes get soaked. So it is best simply to enjoy what I'm seeing rather than go racing off in search of safety.

Another half an hour passes. My grandfather, who was an engineer, liked to teach me the laws of physics while we were out having fun together: 'After a lightning flash, count the seconds before the next peal of thunder and multiply by 340 metres, which is the speed of sound. That way, you'll always know how far off the thunder is.' A little complicated, perhaps, but I've been doing that calculation since I was a child, and I know that, right now, this storm is two kilometres away.

There is still enough light for me to be able to see the shape of the clouds. They are the sort pilots refer to as Cb – cumulonimbus. These are shaped like anvils, as if a blacksmith were hammering the skies, forging swords for furious gods who must, at this moment, be immediately over the town of Tarbes.

I can see the storm approaching. As with any storm, it brings with it destruction, but it also waters the fields; and, with the rain, falls the wisdom of the heavens. As with any storm, it will pass. The more violent the storm, the more quickly it will pass.

I have, thank God, learned to face storms.

Some Final Prayers

Dhammapada (attributed to Buddha)
It would be better if, instead of a thousand words,
There was only one, a word that brought Peace.
It would be better if, instead of a thousand poems,
There was only one, a poem that revealed true Beauty.
It would be better if, instead of a thousand songs,
There was only one, a song that spread Happiness.

Mevlana Jelaluddin Rumi (thirteenth century)
Outside, beyond what is right and wrong, there exists
  a vast field.
We will find each other there.

The Prophet Mohammed (seventh century)
Oh, Allah, I turn to you because you know everything,
  even what is hidden.
If what I am doing is good for me and for my religion,
  for my life now and hereafter, then let that task be
  easy and blessed.
If what I am doing is bad for me and for my religion,
  for my life now and hereafter, remove me from that
  task.

Jesus of Nazareth (Matthew 7: 7–8)

Ask, and it will be given you; seek, and you will find; knock, and it will be opened to you. For everyone who asks receives, and he who seeks finds, and to him who knocks it will be opened.

Jewish Prayer for Peace

Come let us go up to the mountain of the Lord that we may walk in His paths. And we shall beat our swords into ploughshares and our spears into pruning hooks.

Nation shall not lift up sword against nation, neither shall they learn war anymore.

And none shall be afraid, for the mouth of the Lord of Hosts has spoken.

Lao Tsu, China (sixth century BC)

If there is to be peace in the world, the nations must live in peace.

If there is to be peace among nations, the cities must not rise up against each other.

If there is to be peace in the cities, neighbours must understand each other.

If there is to be peace among neighbours, there must be harmony in the home.

If there is to be peace in the home, we must each find our own heart.

More about Paulo Coelho
and Like the Flowing River

Author Biography: Paulo Coelho

Paulo Coelho was born in Rio in August 1947, the son of Pedro Queima Coelho de Souza, an engineer, and his wife Lygia, a homemaker. Early on, Coelho dreamed of an artistic career, something frowned upon in his middle-class household. In the austere surroundings of a strict Jesuit school, Coelho discovered his true vocation: to be a writer. Coelho's parents, however, had different plans for him. When their attempts to suppress his devotion to literature failed, they took it as a sign of mental illness. When Coelho was seventeen, his father twice had him committed to a mental institution, where he endured sessions of electroconvulsive 'therapy'. His parents brought him back to the institution once more, after he became involved with a theatre group and started to work as a journalist.

Coelho was always a nonconformist and a seeker of the new. When, in the excitement of 1968, the guerrilla and hippy movements took hold in a Brazil ruled by a repressive military regime, Coelho embraced progressive politics and joined the peace and love generation. He sought spiritual experiences travelling all over Latin America in the footsteps of Carlos Castaneda. He worked in the theatre and dabbled in journalism, launching an alternative magazine called *2001*. He began to collaborate with music producer Raul Seixas as a lyricist, transforming the Brazilian rock scene. In 1973 Coelho and Raul joined the Alternative Society, an organisation that defended the individual's right to free expression, and began publishing a series of comic strips, calling for more freedom. Members of the organisation were detained and imprisoned. Two days later, Coelho was kidnapped and tortured by a group of paramilitaries.

This experience affected him profoundly. At the age of twenty-six, Coelho decided that he had had enough of living on the edge and wanted to be 'normal'. He worked as an executive in the music industry. He tried his hand at writing but didn't start seriously until after he had an encounter with a stranger. The man first came to him in a vision, and two months later Coelho met him at a café in Amsterdam. The stranger suggested that Coelho should return to Catholicism and study the benign side of magic. He also encouraged Coelho to walk the Road to Santiago, the medieval pilgrim's route.

In 1987 a year after completing that pilgrimage, Coelho wrote *The Pilgrimage*. The book describes his experiences and his discovery that the extraordinary occurs in the lives of ordinary people. A year later, Coelho wrote a very different book, *The Alchemist*. The first edition sold only nine hundred copies and the publishing house decided not to reprint it.

Coelho would not surrender his dream. He found another publishing house, a bigger one. He wrote *Brida* (a work still unpublished in English); the book received a lot of attention in the press, and both *The Alchemist* and *The Pilgrimage* appeared on bestseller lists.

Paulo has gone on to write many other bestselling books, including *The Valkyries, By the River Piedra I Sat Down and Wept, The Fifth Mountain, Warrior of the Light: A Manual, Eleven Minutes, The Zahir* and *The Devil and Miss Prym.*

Today, Paulo Coelho's books appear at the top of bestseller lists worldwide. In 2002 the *Jornal de Letras de Portugal*, the foremost literary authority in the Portuguese language, bestowed upon *The Alchemist* the title of most sold book in the history of the language. In 2003 Coelho's novel *Eleven Minutes* was the world's bestselling fiction title (*USA Today, Publishing Trends*).

In addition to his novels, Coelho writes a globally syndicated weekly newspaper column and occasionally publishes articles on current affairs. His newsletter, *The Manual On-Line*, has over 70,000 subscribers.

Coelho and his wife, Christina Oiticica, are the founders of the Paulo Coelho Institute, which provides support and opportunities for underprivileged members of Brazilian society.

Life is a
journey

Make sure you don't miss a thing.
Live it with Paulo Coelho.

What are you searching for?

A transforming journey on the pilgrims' road to Santiago - and the first of Paulo's extraordinary books.

The Pilgrimage

Do you believe in yourself?

A modern-day adventure in the searing heat of the Mojave desert and an exploration of fear and self-doubt.

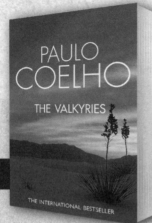

The Valkyries

How can you find your heart's desire?

A world-wide phenomenon; an inspiration for anyone seeking their path in life.

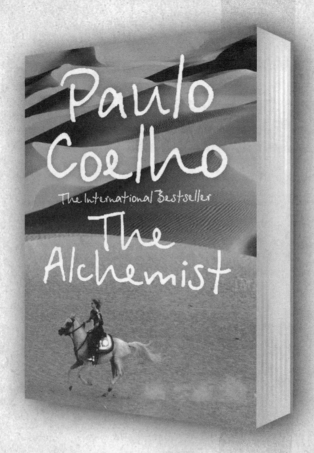

How do we see the amazing in every day?

When two young lovers are reunited, they discover anew the truth of what lies in their hearts.

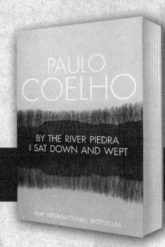

By the River Piedra I Sat Down and Wept

Is life always worth living?

A fundamental moral question explored as only Paulo Coelho can.

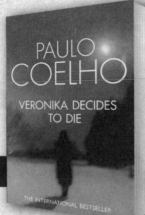

Veronika Decides to Die

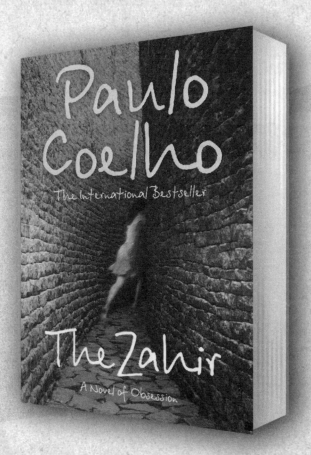

How far would you go for your obsession?

A sweeping story of love, loss and longing that spans the world.

Could you be tempted into evil?

The inhabitants of a small town are challenged by a mysterious stranger to choose between good and evil.

The Devil and Miss Prym

Can faith triumph over suffering?

Paulo Coelho's brilliant telling of the story of Elijah, who was forced to choose between love and duty.

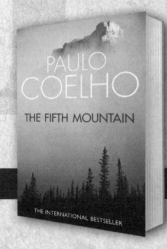

The Fifth Mountain

Can sex be sacred?

An unflinching exploration of the lengths we go to in our search for love, sex and spirituality.

Eleven Minutes

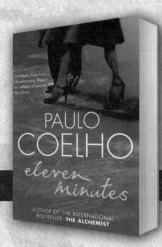

Are you brave enough to live your dream?

Strategies and inspiration to help you follow your own path in a troubled world.

Manual of the Warrior of Light

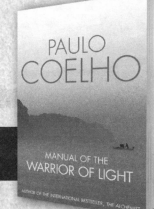

Feeling
inspired?

Discover more about the
world of Paulo Coelho.

Visit his official international website
www.paulocoelho.com